simple, fresh, delicious

recipes for easy living and relaxed entertaining

lovoni walker

photography by merle prosofsky

fabulous food creations inc.

First published by Fabulous Food Creations Inc. in Canada 2005.

Published by Fabulous Food Creations Inc.
1506 – 7 Street, Nisku, Alberta, Canada T9E 7S1
Tel: (780) 955-3841 Fax: (780) 955-3965
Website: www.fabulousfoodcreations.com

Library and Archives Canada Cataloguing in Publication

Walker, Lovoni, 1965–
    Simple, fresh, delicious: recipes for easy living and relaxed
    entertaining / Lovoni Walker ; photography by Merle Prosofsky.

    Includes bibliographical references and index.
    ISBN 0-9737371-0-7

    1. Cookery. I. Prosofsky, Merle, 1955 II. Title.

TX833.5.W34 2005   641.5   C2005-901905-0

Editor: Lee Craig
Editorial Assistant: Rendi Dennis
Proofreader: Stephanie Amodio
Design and Production: John Smith and Kelly Kotyk, Artsmith Communications
Photographer: Merle Prosofsky
Assistant Photographer and Digital Technician: Amanda Stewart, Merle Prosofsky Ltd.
Food Stylist: Lovoni Walker
Writer's Assistant: Shelagh Kubish

Prop Stylist: Snez Ferenac, Distinctive Design
Many, many thanks to our following prop suppliers:
Stokes (780) 440.0370; Mikasa Home Store (780) 438.7274; Pier 1 Imports (780) 432.8177; Rafters Home Store (780) 432.5868; Blyss Decor (780) 424.4522; Architectural Clearinghouse (780) 436-1222; Santa Sweets Inc., Florida www.santasweets.com

ISBN 0-9737371-0-7

Disclaimer
The recipes and contents in this book have been carefully reviewed and tested. For people with food allergies or people who have special food requirements or health issues, please read each recipe carefully to determine whether or not it may cause a health problem for you. All the information and recipes contained in this cookbook are used at the risk of the consumer. The publisher and author cannot be responsible for any hazards, damage or health issues that may occur as the result of any of the subject matter contained in this cookbook. This is not a medical or health cookbook. Its contents are intended to provide general information. It is up to the reader to determine if the contents may have an adverse effect for the reader.

Also by Lovoni Walker:
The Essential Canadian Christmas Cookbook by Lone Pine Publishing
The Essential Christmas Cookbook by Lone Pine Publishing

Printed in Singapore by Star Standard Industries PTE LTD.

For Scott &
Mum, John, Debbie,
Ray & Emily

with all my love

acknowledgements

As I tested the recipes in this cookbook and prepared them for photography, I watched the house behind our place being built. Every day there would be a little more progress on the house, and someone else there working on it. It actually takes less time to build a house than it does to create a cookbook, but both rely on a team of people to make it all come together. Without these people, this cookbook would still be a mere dream, so I want to thank everyone from the bottom of my heart—you all made it happen.

My thanks go to all these incredible people: to Scott, for all that you are and all that you do, how blessed I am to have you in my life; without your emotional and financial support this cookbook never would have happened, and there is no way I can ever thank you enough. To my cousin, Robert, thanks for taking the time to talk to me across the miles, helping me put together the business plan. Merle, thank you for giving my recipes life. The images are fantastic, and it is always such fun working with you. Amanda, thanks for all your hard work and your insatiable interest in food, I never grow tired of answering your questions. Mary Anne, thank you for washing up my dishes and ironing and for your feedback, support and encouragement. Snez, prop stylist and my friend, you helped to keep me sane during this project; thank you so much. John Smith, you brought my vision and dream to life and designed such a beautiful cookbook; it is always such a delight working with you; thank you.

Kelly, talented and patient with me, what a combination; thank you so much for your hard work. Lee, thanks for your attention to detail, going the extra mile and being so patient with me through the whole process. Rendi, how you managed to decipher all that scribble and make sense of all our editing notes, I will never know, but I owe you a big thanks. Ross, you saw potential in my project and in me, and I will always be grateful to you for that, so many thanks to you. Thanks to my wonderful sister, Debbie. Your incredible contribution helped to make this happen; you knew how much writing this book meant to me and I will always be grateful to you. Thanks also to my brother-in-law, Ray, because I know you supported the whole idea. Marie, thank you so much for your financial support and your encouragement. Thanks to Steph for your keen eye proofing and your friendship; working with you is always such fun. Thanks to Derrick for your advice and expertise and for being such a dear friend. Many thanks to Janice at Star Standard Printing for the amazing service. Thanks to Shelagh for your writing contributions. Thanks to Audrey for helping me out on some of your days off. Many thanks to the Business Development Bank of Canada and a special thanks to Dawn and Angela there. Last but never least, my parents: thank you, Mum, for always encouraging me to do whatever I set my mind to, for instilling in me the courage to have faith in myself, to aim for the stars and never doubt myself; to John, my father, for opening a child's eyes at such a young age to so many wonderful foods of the world; I am sure you planted the seed that led me to this incredible career that I love so much.

Thank-you x.

contents

introduction

I love good food. Actually, it's more a passion I have with both food and cooking. I have always eaten well and enjoyed the best food nature has to offer thanks to my family's love of food and cooking. I was raised on good, wholesome food, and as a child I was exposed to a wide selection of ethnic ingredients from around the globe. How lucky we are today to have such an incredible array of food from every part of this planet so readily available. We are surrounded by fresh, nourishing food that can be prepared in no time with a minimum of fuss, but many people think that preparing tasty, healthy food is time-consuming, complicated or expensive. We are led to believe by clever marketing and advertising that having such busy lives means we don't have time to cook for ourselves or our families. We are often made to think that we will save time opening a package and heating its contents in the microwave. Do you know you can have a wonderful, nutritious meal on the table faster than it takes to cook a frozen pizza?

As so many of us rush through today's busy lifestyle, we are often not preparing and eating nutritious, well-balanced meals. I hope this cookbook will encourage people to eat better and show that good, healthy food doesn't mean skimping on flavour or using complicated methods. Preparing good food isn't time-consuming, and it can be very simple and rewarding. Eating fresh food that tastes good and fuels your body can help the way we think, the way we look and our moods. It can determine our health and well-being, so why wouldn't you want to nourish your body and mind?

simple, fresh, delicious, the first cookbook in the *simple, delicious* series, focuses on fresh ingredients, fresh ideas and easy-to-prepare recipes. Whether you're an experienced cook looking for some new ideas or a novice wanting to learn, I hope you are inspired by the recipes in this cookbook. I have used an abundance of the best mother nature has to offer by adding layers of fragrant dimensions to the recipes with fresh herbs, spices, citrus and garlic. The flavour of the fresh foods has been allowed to shine and take centre stage.

The recipes in this cookbook cover everything from breakfast to dessert with a useful section called *basics and essentials*. This section has recipes to get you stocking-up your kitchen with what you need to make prep time quick and easy. It includes recipes such as mayonnaise, stewed tomatoes, pesto and broths and explanations of basic kitchen steps, such as how to toasts nuts and bruise garlic. Make these foods yourself or buy them ready-made from the store; the choice is yours.

Use this cookbook as a tool. Get it dog-eared and dirty. Use it to plan your weekly meals or to help you organize casual gatherings on the weekend with friends. Most of the recipes are marked "30 minutes or less" or "make ahead" to help you plan at a glance. Write out a shopping list before you head out to the store—it will save you time and money.

I encourage you to support your local producers when you can and to shop at farmers' markets. Buy produce in season. Fresh, in-season produce tastes better, is nutritionally better for you and is cheaper than buying produce out of season. Perhaps buy some produce you haven't bought before and experiment. Don't ever be afraid of preparing foods you haven't cooked before—it's all an adventure. Never be afraid to insist on better quality and variety in the grocery stores you shop in. I am sure if it's within reason the stores will comply and do their best to accommodate your wishes.

Share recipes with friends, eat with your family and teach and encourage your children to cook. Whether you have lots of time or limited time, enjoy cooking and eating good food. Cook fresh, simple and delicious food because you and the people you care about are worth that. Feed yourself and others well by nourishing the body and soul. Eat well, eat fresh and enjoy—you deserve it.

kitchen info

All bakeware and ingredients are measured in metric. The imperial conversions are approximations.

All the recipes in this cookbook have been carefully tested and every endeavour has been made to ensure their accuracy, but please note, cooking times are approximate and may vary according to the different ovens, pots and pans being used.

Around the world we have different names for different products:

Red and green peppers—capsicum
Cilantro—coriander
Sweet potato (yam)—kumara
Romaine lettuce—cos lettuce
Butternut squash—butternut pumpkin
Eggplant—aubergine
Zucchini—cougette
Rutabaga—swede
Arugula—rocket
Ground beef and chicken—
    minced beef and chicken
Shrimp—prawns
Broiler—grill
Whole-wheat—wholemeal
Sliced almonds—flaked almonds
All-purpose flour—plain flour
Baking soda—soda bicarbonate
Parchment paper—baking paper

In this cookbook:

Ground beef is lean
Honey is liquid
Milk is 2%
Sour cream is light
Yogurt is 3.25%
Eggs are large
Flour is unbleached
Brown sugar is dark brown
Parsley is flat leaf (Italian)
Salt is sea salt
Pepper is freshly ground black pepper
Lemon, lime and orange juice are fresh

1 teaspoon = 5ml
1 tablespoon = 15ml (Canada, USA, UK)
1 cup = 250ml

When using raw egg whites, ensure the freshness of the eggs. It is advisable not to feed raw egg whites and some soft cheese varieties to the elderly, children or pregnant and nursing mothers.

basics and essentials

The foundation of good cooking is having essential pantry items on hand. Toast, roast, cook, blend. Prepare your own staples ahead to make meal times easier. Good food starts fresh.

roasted peppers

In this basic recipe I am only giving you an example of how many peppers you can roast at one time. Roast as little or as many peppers as you wish! Any coloured peppers can be used. One pepper will yield about 1/2 cup of sliced pepper.

4 large red peppers
4 large yellow peppers
olive oil, plus extra
salt and freshly ground pepper

Preheat a broiler, barbecue or grill pan to medium-high heat.

Brush the peppers with the oil and place on a baking sheet. Roast under the preheated broiler, turning occasionally, for about 10 minutes or until the skin is blistered and blackened. Place in a large bowl, cover and let stand for 10 minutes.

Peel away and discard the skin from the peppers. Cut open each pepper and scrape out and discard the seeds and membranes. Cut the peppers into thin strips. Place into an airtight container add some oil (about 1 to 3 tablespoons) and a pinch of salt and pepper. Store in the fridge until ready to use.

Make ahead: The peppers can be made 2 weeks ahead and stored in an airtight container in the fridge. Let stand at room temperature for about 30 minutes before serving. Drain from the oil before use.

Serving suggestion: Add the peppers to salads, soups, sandwiches and pizza toppings or serve them as part of an antipasto platter. To add to a sauce, put them into a blender or food processor and process until smooth.

make ahead

segmenting oranges and grapefruit

The reason for segmenting grapefruit and oranges is to release the succulent flesh between the membranes.

To segment oranges and grapefruit, cut both ends from the fruit.

Place the fruit cut-side down on a cutting board. Using a utility or paring knife, cut down and around the fruit, following the shape of the fruit and removing as much of the white pith with the skin as possible.

Place a bowl underneath the fruit to catch any juice. Cut between the membranes of each segment and let them drop into the bowl.

Make ahead: The segments can be prepared a day ahead and stored in an airtight container in the fridge.

Serving suggestion: Segmented oranges and grapefruit can be used in fruit salads, desserts and savoury salads.

roasted peppers

segmenting oranges and grapefruit

stewed tomatoes

stewed tomatoes

Use these in place of canned tomatoes; they have less salt and a lot more flavour. Make up a batch and freeze to have on hand. Remember, the better the tomatoes, the better the end result, so choose red, juicy tomatoes.

14 medium ripe tomatoes (about 6 lbs/3kg)
1 tablespoon olive oil
3 cups chopped onion (about 3 medium onions)
10 garlic cloves, minced
5.6 oz (156ml) can tomato paste
2 teaspoons balsamic vinegar
1 teaspoon packed brown sugar
salt and freshly ground pepper

Remove and discard the stem end from each tomato. Make an X on the bottom of each tomato with a small sharp knife.

Bring a large pot of water to a boil. Carefully put the tomatoes into the water and simmer for 30 to 60 seconds or until the skin is just starting to peel away. Remove from the pot and place into a large bowl of iced water to stop the cooking. Let stand for 5 minutes and then drain.

Peel away and discard the skins. Chop the tomatoes into large chunks.

Heat the oil in a large pot or Dutch oven over medium-high heat. Add the onion and cook, stirring occasionally, for about 5 minutes or until softened. Stir in the garlic and cook for about 1 minute or until fragrant.

Add the tomatoes and remaining ingredients and stir until well combined. Increase the heat to high. Bring to a boil and then reduce the heat to medium. Boil gently, uncovered, stirring occasionally, for about 45 minutes or until thickened.

Store the stewed tomatoes in 1 cup and 2 cup airtight containers. Label each container with the contents, quantity and date; seal and freeze.

Make ahead: The tomatoes can be made a week ahead and stored in an airtight container in the fridge. Or store them in the freezer for up to 6 months.

Serving suggestion: Use in pasta, lasagna, soups, curries, casseroles and stews.

Makes about 9 cups   make ahead

chicken broth

chicken broth

Making your own chicken broth is easy and inexpensive, and it contains less salt than most commercially prepared broths, although the packages of prepared broth are convenient to have on hand in the pantry. To make the broth, all you have to do is throw everything in a pot and let it simmer away for a few hours. I like to add lots of vegetables to mine because I find they add to the flavour.

1 bunch parsley
3 lbs (1.5kg) whole chicken
2 onions, with peel, quartered
4 large carrots, chopped
4 celery stalks, chopped
8 garlic cloves, bruised (see page 22 for tips)
3 bay leaves
1 tablespoon whole black peppercorns
salt
4 quarts (4 litres) water

Cut the stems from the parsley and put them into a stock pot or large Dutch oven. Reserve the parsley leaves for another use.

Rinse the chicken inside and out with cold water and add to the pot.

Add the remaining ingredients and bring to a boil over high heat; reduce the heat to medium-low. Simmer, uncovered, for 3 hours. Skim-off and discard any residue from the surface as the broth cooks.

Cool the broth slightly before straining it through a fine metal sieve into a large heatproof bowl; discard the solids. Cover the broth with plastic wrap and place in the fridge for 8 hours or overnight.

Carefully scrape and discard any fat from the surface of the broth. Store the broth in 1/2 cup, 1 cup, 2 cup and 1 quart (1 litre) airtight containers. Label each container with the contents, quantity and date; seal and freeze.

Make ahead: The broth can be made 3 days ahead and stored in an airtight container in the fridge. Or store it in the freezer for up to 6 months.

Serving suggestion: Use the broth as a base for soups and add to stews, sauces and rice dishes.

Makes about 3 quarts (3 litres)   make ahead

cooking legumes

This method is the same regardless of which dried beans you are using — chick peas, kidney beans, small white beans, black-eyed peas, etc. The cooking times will vary, however, so it is important to keep testing for doneness as the legumes cook. You don't want to overcook them. Two cups of cooked legumes are about equivalent to a 19 oz (540ml) can.

**1 1/2 lb (750g) package (about 3 1/2 cups)
dried legumes, such as chick peas,
small white beans, kidney beans, etc.**

Place the legumes in an extra-large bowl and add enough cold water to cover them by about 4 inches (10cm). Cover and let stand at room temperature for 8 hours or overnight; drain.

Place the drained legumes in a large pot or Dutch oven. Add enough water to cover them by about 4 inches (10cm).

Bring to a boil and then reduce the heat to medium. Cook, uncovered, for 30 to 60 minutes, depending on the variety of legumes you are cooking, or until tender but not mushy.

Let the legumes cool before storing. Store them in 1 and 2 cup quantities in resealable bags or airtight containers. Label each bag with the contents, quantity and date; seal and freeze.

Make ahead: The legumes can be cooked 3 days ahead and stored in airtight containers in the fridge. Or freeze them for up to 3 months.

Serving suggestion: Have legumes on hand to add to soups, stews, curries, salads and dips.

Makes about 8 cups   make ahead

vegetable broth

vegetable broth

Using a good vegetable broth instead of water adds significantly more flavour to vegetable-based soups, stews and sauces.

4 medium carrots, chopped
2 large onions, chopped
4 celery stalks, chopped
4 garlic cloves, chopped
2 cups sliced mushrooms (5 1/2 oz/170g)
2 bay leaves
3 thyme sprigs
1 tablespoon whole black peppercorns
2 cups dry white wine
2 1/2 quarts (2.5 litres) water
salt

Combine all the ingredients in a large pot or Dutch oven and stir. Bring to a boil and then reduce the heat to medium-low.

Simmer, uncovered, for 1 hour.

Cool the broth slightly before straining it through a fine metal sieve into a large bowl; discard the solids. Store the broth in 1/2 cup, 1 cup, 2 cup and 1 quart (1 litre) airtight containers. Label each container with the contents, quantity and date; seal and freeze.

Make ahead: The broth can be made a week ahead and stored in airtight containers in the fridge. Or store in the freezer for up to 6 months.

Serving suggestion: Use in soups, stews, sauces and rice dishes.

Makes about 2 quarts (2 litres)　　　　　make ahead

making fresh breadcrumbs

basil pesto

mayonnaise

cooking rice

making fresh breadcrumbs

Fresh breadcrumbs make an excellent coating on fish, chicken, veal, pork, shrimp, calamari and vegetables. They add texture and help to retain the juices in the meat when baked or fried. When added to patties or meatballs, they help bind the ingredients together. When processed coarsely, the breadcrumbs can be made into stuffing for chicken, turkey, pork and red meats.

Breadcrumbs are also a good way of using up any uneaten or stale bread. Use your choice of breads such as multi-grain. You can remove the crusts from the bread first, but I prefer to use the crusts, too.

1 1/4 lb (625g)* bread loaf, cut into chunks

Put the bread into a food processor in batches and process until fine crumbs (if you are making breadcrumbs for a stuffing, process into coarse crumbs).

Place them in a large resealable bag or an airtight container and freeze for up to 3 months. Let them thaw before using. Use the breadcrumbs as required.

Make ahead: The breadcrumbs can be made a week ahead and stored in an airtight container or a resealable plastic bag in a cool, dry place. Or store them in the freezer for up to 6 months.

* Bread loaves vary in weight.

Makes about 6 cups   make ahead

basil pesto

Traditionally, pesto is made with a mortar and pestle, but I prefer the convenience of a food processor. You can buy good-quality bottled pesto, but try making your own when the basil is in season and plentiful. Experiment with other herbs such as mint, coriander (cilantro) and arugula.

2 cups fresh basil leaves
1/2 cup pine nuts, toasted (see page 22 for tips)
1/2 cup finely grated, fresh parmesan cheese
2 garlic cloves, chopped
salt and freshly ground pepper
1/3 cup olive oil, plus about 1 tablespoon extra

Put the basil, pine nuts, parmesan cheese, garlic and a pinch of salt and pepper into a food processor bowl and process until combined.

With the motor running, add the oil in a slow, steady stream down the feed shoot until well combined and the mixture forms a paste.

Store in airtight containers. Drizzle the top of the pesto with the extra oil to prevent discoloration.

Make ahead: The pesto can be made a week ahead and stored in an airtight container in the fridge.

Serving suggestion: Add the pesto to pasta, meatballs, soups, stews, casseroles and toasted sandwiches.

Makes about 1 1/2 cups   30 minutes or less

mayonnaise

The mayonnaise can be flavoured with herbs, horseradish, sweet chili sauce, spices and, of course, garlic.

3 egg yolks
1 1/2 tablespoons lemon juice
1 1/2 tablespoons white wine vinegar
1/2 teaspoon granulated sugar
salt
1 1/2 cups vegetable oil or light olive oil

Line a baking sheet with parchment paper. Preheat the oven to 400°F (200°C).

Put the yolks, juice, vinegar, sugar and a pinch of salt in a food processor and process until smooth.

With the motor running, add the oil in a slow, steady stream down the feed shoot until the mixture is thick and pale. This step should take about 4 minutes.

Make ahead: The mayonnaise can be made 4 days ahead and stored in an airtight container in the fridge.

Serving suggestion: Serve a small spoonful of mayonnaise on top of seafood soup and stews, on sandwiches, in egg salad and potato salad and as a base for coleslaw dressing and tartar sauce.

Makes about 1 2/3 cups   30 minutes or less

cooking rice

Some simple things can be the most challenging — like cooking rice. I think this is a foolproof method, one that was taught to me by my father, whose rice always seems to be cooked to perfection. For the best flavour I generally use jasmine rice or rinsed basmati rice.

2 1/4 cups water
1 1/2 cups jasmine rice
salt

Bring the water to a boil in a medium (2 quart/2 litre) saucepan with a heavy base over a small burner or hot plate.

Stir in the rice and a pinch of salt. Reduce the heat to low (as low as the burner will go). Cover tightly and cook for 20 minutes. Remove from the heat and fluff the rice with a fork. Serve hot.

Make ahead: The rice is best made just before serving.

Serving suggestion: Serve as an accompaniment to curries, stews, chilies and soups. Or rinse the cooked rice under cold water, drain well and add to salads.

Makes about 5 cups   30 minutes or less

bruising garlic

Bruising partially crushes the garlic cloves, releasing a subtle flavour. This method is also an easy way to remove the skin from the individual cloves.

Place an unpeeled garlic clove on a cutting board and press down firmly with the flat blade of a knife or the smooth side of a meat mallet until the clove is slightly squashed.

Make ahead: It is best to bruise garlic just before serving.

Serving suggestion: Add to roasted vegetables and meat for a subtle flavour. Remove the cloves before serving.

toasting nuts

Toasting brings out the best flavour of nuts. I prefer to toast nuts in the oven because I find they brown more evenly. For smaller amounts, place the nuts into a small frying pan and stir over medium heat until golden. For anything over 1/2 cup, I generally use the oven though. If I am toasting nuts for one recipe, I tend to toast a batch, use what I need, let the extra nuts cool and then store them in the freezer. That way I always have some on hand. Nuts can burn easily, so always set the timer and keep your eye on them.

Preheat the oven to 350°F (180°C).

Place the nuts on a baking sheet. Toast in the preheated oven for 5 to 10 minutes, depending on the nut and quantity being toasted, or until golden brown.

If storing the nuts, let them cool completely before storing them in airtight containers or resealable bags.

Make ahead: Nuts can be stored in airtight containers in the freezer for up to 3 months.

Serving suggestion: Toasted nuts can be used almost anywhere: in salads, cakes, muffins and stuffings, sprinkled on yogurt and ice cream, in stir-fries, stirred through rice and couscous, on sandwiches and in wraps.

bruising garlic

toasting nuts

Many years ago I tried a sticky date dessert cake recipe, and even today it is still a favourite of mine. I have made variations to the recipe over time and here is another, with the addition of pears and pecans. It is incredibly moist and delicious.

1 1/4 cups water
1 cup pitted dates
1 teaspoon baking soda
1/4 cup softened butter
2/3 cup packed brown sugar
2 eggs
1 cup all-purpose flour
2 teaspoons baking powder
1/2 cup coarsely chopped pecans
1 large pear, peeled, cored and chopped

Grease a 9 x 5 x 3 inch (23 x 13 x 8cm) loaf pan and line the base and long sides with parchment paper. Preheat the oven to 350°F (180°C).

Combine the water and dates in a medium saucepan. Bring the mixture to a boil, uncovered, over high heat. Immediately remove it from the heat and stir in the baking soda (the mixture will froth). Cool for 10 minutes.

Using an electric mixer, beat the butter, sugar, eggs, flour, baking powder and date mixture in a large bowl until combined. Stir in the remaining ingredients.

Pour the mixture into the prepared pan. Bake in the preheated oven for about 40 minutes or until a skewer inserted into the centre of the loaf comes out clean. Let stand in the pan for 10 minutes before turning the loaf out onto a wire rack to cool. Cut into 12 slices. Serve warm or at room temperature. Cool completely before storing.

Make ahead: Wrap each slice individually in plastic wrap, place in an airtight container and freeze for up to 1 month.

Serving suggestion: Serve with fresh fruit and tea or coffee.

Makes 12 slices   make ahead

date, pear and pecan loaf

banana cranberry muffins

banana cranberry muffins

The riper the bananas you use in this recipe, the better the muffins will be. It is a good idea to freeze any bananas that are past their prime to have on hand for banana bread, muffins and cakes.

2 cups all-purpose flour
4 teaspoons baking powder
1 1/2 teaspoons ground ginger
1/2 teaspoon ground cinnamon
1/2 cup packed brown sugar
1/2 cup dried cranberries (or craisins)
1/2 cup chopped walnuts, toasted (see page 22 for tips)
1 1/2 cups mashed banana (about 4 medium bananas)
3 eggs
1/2 cup buttermilk
1/4 cup vegetable oil

Grease a 12 hole muffin pan. Preheat the oven to 375°F (190°C).

Sift the flour, baking powder, ginger and cinnamon into a large bowl. Add the sugar, cranberries and walnuts and stir until combined.

Whisk the remaining ingredients together in a medium bowl and add to the flour mixture. Stir until the mixture just comes together; do not overmix. Spoon the mixture into the prepared pan.

Bake in the preheated oven for 20 to 25 minutes or until a skewer inserted into the centre of a muffin comes out clean. Let stand in the pan for 5 minutes before turning muffins out onto a wire rack. Serve warm. Cool completely before storing.

Make ahead: Wrap each muffin individually in plastic wrap and then place them in a resealable plastic bag and freeze for up to 1 month. Reheat in the microwave until thawed and warm.

Serving suggestion: Serve with the **watermelon and grapefruit slushie** (page 37).

Makes 12   make ahead

maple muesli

This recipe makes a generous amount suitable for about 20 helpings. You can easily halve it if you don't wish to make so much. Store it in an airtight jar or in the freezer to keep it fresh. As well as breakfast, also try it for a quick snack in the mid afternoon if you are craving something with some crunch and a little sweetness.

3 egg whites
1 cup maple syrup
1 1/2 teaspoons ground cinnamon
salt
4 cups rolled oats (old-fashioned oats)
1 cup pumpkin (pepita) seed kernels
1 cup sunflower seed kernels
1 cup sliced almonds
1 cup pecan pieces
1/3 cup sesame seeds

Grease 2 large baking sheets. Preheat the oven to 375°F (190°C).

Whisk the egg whites, maple syrup, cinnamon and a pinch of salt in an extra-large bowl until well combined.

Add the remaining ingredients and stir until well coated.

Spread the oat mixture onto the prepared baking sheets. Bake in the preheated oven, stirring occasionally, for about 25 minutes or until golden brown and crisp. Let cool completely before storing.

Make ahead: The muesli can be stored up to 1 month in airtight jars.

Serving suggestion: Serve with milk and sliced fresh pear, strawberries or banana. Or try it with **apple and dried fruit compote** (page 32) and yogurt.

Makes about 10 cups ❁ make ahead

Try this compote with yogurt or have it on your breakfast cereal. It also makes a wonderful dessert served with frozen yogurt or ice cream.

2 medium green apples, peeled, cored and chopped
1 cup pitted prunes
1 cup pitted dates
1 cup dried apricots, halved
1 1/2 cups apple juice
2 tablespoons honey
1/4 teaspoon ground cinnamon

Combine all the ingredients in a medium saucepan over medium heat and bring to a gentle boil. Cook, uncovered, stirring occasionally, for 5 to 10 minutes or until the apples are softened (the mixture will thicken upon cooling).

Make ahead: The compote can be made 5 days ahead and stored in an airtight container in the fridge.

Serving suggestion: Serve with yogurt or cereal.

Makes about 4 cups   30 minutes or less   make ahead

apple and dried fruit compote

berry lime salad

berry lime salad

If fresh berries aren't in season, then use thawed frozen berries. To thaw the berries, spread them onto baking sheets lined with paper towel and place them in the fridge until thawed. This recipe also makes a wonderful dessert served with ice cream.

2 cups fresh raspberries
2 cups fresh blueberries
2 cups fresh sliced strawberries
1 tablespoon finely grated lime zest
2 tablespoons lime juice
3 tablespoons granulated sugar
1 tablespoon balsamic vinegar

Put all the ingredients in a large bowl and gently stir to combine. Cover and place in the fridge for 1 to 3 hours to allow the flavours to develop. Or the berries can be served immediately.

Make ahead: The salad can be made a day ahead and stored, covered, in the fridge. The berries will break down and become delicious and syrupy.

Serving suggestion: Serve with vanilla yogurt.

Serves 4 to 6   30 minutes or less   make ahead

watermelon and grapefruit slushie

baked apricots with ricotta and maple

watermelon and grapefruit slushie

The combination of the sweetness of the watermelon and the tartness of the grapefruit is a wonderful morning pick-me-up.

1 cup grapefruit juice
2 cups chopped watermelon
8 ice cubes

Put all the ingredients into a blender and blend until smooth.

Make ahead: The slushie is best made just before serving.

Serving suggestion: This slushie also makes a wonderful cocktail with the addition of sparkling wine or vodka.

Makes about 3 1/2 cups   30 minutes or less

baked apricots with ricotta and maple

Fresh apricots are in season for only a short time, so use canned apricots packed in natural juice at other times. If you are using canned apricots, drain them well on paper towel to absorb any excess juice. The size of the apricots in the cans vary between each brand.

12 medium ripe apricots, halved and pit removed
   (or 2 x 14 oz/398ml cans, drained)
1 tablespoon melted butter
8 oz (250g) ricotta cheese
2 tablespoons maple syrup
2 tablespoons sliced almonds

Grease a medium shallow baking dish. Preheat the oven to 400°F (200°C).

Place the apricots, cut side up, in the prepared dish. Brush the cut side of the apricots with the melted butter.

Spoon the ricotta cheese onto each apricot half and drizzle with the maple syrup. Sprinkle with the almonds.

Bake, uncovered, in the preheated oven for about 20 minutes or until the almonds are turning golden brown. Serve warm.

Make ahead: The apricots are best made just before serving.

Serves 6   30 minutes or less

salmon, asparagus and egg with dill butter

salmon, asparagus and egg with dill butter

This simple recipe requires having everything ready at once, so have all your ingredients prepared before you start cooking. Ask your fishmonger to remove the skin from the salmon if you prefer it served skinless.

1 teaspoon vegetable oil
12 oz (375g) salmon, cut into 4 pieces
salt and freshly ground pepper
2 tablespoons butter
2 tablespoons lemon juice
2 tablespoons chopped fresh dill
20 asparagus spears, trimmed of woody ends
2 tablespoons white vinegar
4 eggs

Brush the oil over the salmon and sprinkle with salt and pepper. Heat a large frying pan, preferably non-stick, over medium-high heat. Cook the salmon for about 3 minutes on each side, depending on the thickness of the salmon, until just cooked; do not overcook. Remove the salmon to a heatproof plate; cover it with foil and place in a warm oven.

Heat the butter in the same frying pan over medium heat until melted. Stir in the juice, dill and a pinch of salt and pepper. Cover and set aside to keep warm.

Place the asparagus in a large steamer and cook, covered, over simmering water for about 3 minutes or until bright green and crisp.

While the asparagus is cooking, bring about 2 inches (5cm) of water to a simmer in a medium frying pan over medium heat. Stir in the vinegar and then carefully break the eggs into the simmering water. Cook for 2 to 3 minutes or until cooked to your liking.

To assemble, arrange the asparagus, salmon and eggs on a serving plate and drizzle with the warm butter mixture.

Make ahead: This recipe is best made just before serving.

Serves 4   30 minutes or less

The trick to making good scrambled eggs is to not overcook them. Cook the eggs until they are almost set; the residual heat will continue to cook them to perfection. If chives are unavailable, then use finely sliced green onions instead. This recipe can easily be doubled to serve more people.

1 teaspoon butter, plus 1/2 teaspoon extra
8 oz (250g) small button mushrooms, halved
salt and freshly ground pepper
1 teaspoon balsamic vinegar
2 tablespoons chopped fresh chives
4 eggs
1 tablespoon water
2 tablespoons grated smoked cheese (such as applewood)

Melt 1 teaspoon of the butter in a medium frying pan over medium-high heat. Add the mushrooms and a pinch of salt and pepper and cook, stirring occasionally, for about 5 minutes or until the mushrooms are lightly browned.

Add the vinegar and chives and stir until the vinegar is almost evaporated.

While the mushrooms are cooking, whisk the eggs, water and a pinch of salt in a medium bowl until well combined.

Heat the extra butter in a medium frying pan, preferably non-stick, over medium-high heat. Add the egg mixture and cook, stirring occasionally, for 1 to 2 minutes or until almost set.

Remove from heat and stir in the smoked cheese. Serve the scrambled eggs with the mushrooms.

Make ahead: This recipe is best made just before serving.

Serving suggestion: Serve with **watermelon and grapefruit slushie** (page 37) and wholegrain toast.

Serves 2   30 minutes or less

pea and ham tarts

These crustless tarts will puff up as they cook and then deflate on cooling. They also make a delicious lunch served with a salad.

2 teaspoons olive oil
1 cup finely chopped onion (about 1 medium onion)
3/4 cup chopped ham
3/4 cup frozen peas
10 eggs
1/2 cup milk
1/3 cup grated white cheddar cheese
salt and freshly ground pepper

Grease 8, 1/2 cup (4 oz/125 ml) capacity ramekins and place them on a baking sheet. Preheat the oven to 350°F (180°C).

Heat the oil in a medium frying pan over medium-high heat. Add the onion and cook, stirring occasionally, for about 5 minutes or until softened.

Stir in the ham and peas. Divide the mixture evenly into the prepared ramekins.

Whisk the remaining ingredients in a medium bowl until well combined. Pour into the prepared ramekins until each is about three-quarters full.

Bake in the preheated oven for about 20 minutes or until the tarts are set. Serve warm.

Make ahead: The tarts can be prepared up to 3 hours ahead and stored, covered in plastic wrap, in the fridge. Bake them just before serving.

Serving suggestion: Serve with **roasted feta tomatoes** (page 47).

Serves 8   30 minutes or less

smoked cheese scrambled eggs with mushrooms

pea and ham tarts

potato pancakes with corn and bacon

If you prefer food spicy, increase the amount of pepper sauce or serve extra sauce on the side.

2 large russet potatoes (about 2 lbs/1kg), peeled
2 eggs
salt and freshly ground pepper
olive oil, plus 2 teaspoons extra
1/3 cup thinly sliced green onion
1/2 cup chopped back bacon
1 1/2 cups frozen or fresh corn kernels
    (or 14 oz/398ml can, drained)
24 cherry (or grape) tomatoes, halved if large
2 tablespoons chopped fresh cilantro (coriander)
1/2 teaspoon pepper sauce (such as Tobasco)

Grate the potatoes into a fine metal sieve over a medium bowl. Press as much liquid from them as possible.

Whisk the eggs in a medium bowl. Add the potatoes and a pinch of salt and pepper and stir until well combined.

Drizzle a little oil in a large pan, preferably non-stick, and heat over medium-high heat. Drop 1/4 cup of loosely packed potato mixture into the pan, about 2 1/2 inches (6cm) apart, and spread each to about 3 inches (8cm) in diameter. Cook the pancakes in batches, for 3 to 4 minutes on each side or until golden brown. Place the cooked potatoes on a plate lined with paper towel and put them into a warm oven. Heat a drizzle of the oil to the pan before repeating with remaining potato mixture.

While the patties are cooking, heat the extra oil in a large frying pan over medium-high heat. Add the onion, bacon and corn and cook, stirring occasionally, for about 5 minutes or until the onion is softened and the mixture is hot.

Add the tomatoes and cook, stirring occasionally, for about 2 minutes or until they are hot and wilted slightly.

Add the cilantro, sauce and a pinch of salt and pepper and stir until combined. Serve warm with the pancakes.

Make ahead: This recipe is best made just before serving.

Serving suggestion: Serve with sour cream or plain yogurt.

Serves 6

Don't limit this frittata to just brunch; try serving it cold with a salad for lunch or as a light evening meal. Or, cut it into thin wedges and serve it cold as an appetizer.

3 cups chopped sweet potato (yam), (about 1 lb/500g)
2 teaspoons olive oil, plus 2 teaspoons extra
salt and freshly ground pepper
1 1/2 cups thinly sliced onion (about 1 large onion)
1 cup finely chopped back bacon
3 oz (90g) goat cheese, crumbled
10 eggs
2 tablespoons chopped fresh thyme (or parsley)
salt and freshly ground pepper
1/4 cup finely grated, fresh parmesan cheese

Line a baking sheet with parchment paper. Preheat the oven to 400°F (200°C).

Combine the sweet potato, 2 teaspoons of the oil and a pinch of salt and pepper on the prepared baking sheet. Roast in the preheated oven, stirring once, for about 30 minutes or until tender.

While the sweet potato is cooking, heat the extra oil in a large frying pan, preferably non-stick, over medium-high heat. Add the onion and bacon and cook, stirring occasionally, for about 5 minutes or until the onion is softened.

Add the roasted sweet potato and stir until well combined. Scatter the goat cheese over the top.

Whisk the eggs, thyme and a pinch of salt and pepper together in a medium bowl. Pour over the sweet potato and swirl the pan to make sure the egg mixture is evenly distributed. Cook over medium heat for about 5 minutes or until the bottom is golden brown.

Sprinkle with the parmesan cheese. Place under a hot broiler for about 2 minutes or until the top is golden and set. Let stand in the pan for 5 minutes before inverting onto a plate and cutting into wedges. Serve warm or cold.

Make ahead: The frittata can be made 2 days ahead and stored, covered, in the fridge.

Serves 6 to 8   make ahead

roasted sweet potato and bacon frittata

roasted feta tomatoes

roasted feta tomatoes

For the best flavour use lovely red, ripe tomatoes.

3 cups grape (or cherry) tomatoes, halved if large
1 tablespoon olive oil
2 tablespoons chopped fresh oregano
2 teaspoons balsamic vinegar
salt and freshly ground pepper
3 oz (90g) feta cheese, coarsely crumbled

Grease a baking sheet. Preheat the oven to 400°F (200°C).

Toss the tomatoes, oil, oregano, vinegar and a pinch of salt and pepper together on the prepared baking sheet. Bake, uncovered, in the preheated oven for 5 minutes.

Sprinkle the feta cheese over the tomatoes and toss. Roast, uncovered, for 3 to 5 minutes or until the tomatoes are wilted and the cheese is softened.

Make ahead: This recipe is best made just before serving.

Serving suggestion: Serve on thick slices of buttered wholegrain bread.

Serves 4   30 minutes or less

soups, salads, sandwiches

Warm your heart with wholesome food—
crusty baguettes, bowls of steaming hot soup
or eat light and enjoy fresh, crisp salads.
Treat yourself for lunch or entertain good friends.

curried chicken and mango wraps

curried chicken and mango wraps

These wraps are incredibly delicious, and they are now one of my lunch-time favourites. I also find they make a quick evening meal, too. For lunch, prepare the ingredients the night before and assemble them just before serving. Use leftover roasted chicken or buy a roasted chicken from the grocery store.

2 tablespoons mayonnaise
   (your own, see page 21, or store bought)
1/2 teaspoon curry powder
2 large whole-wheat tortillas
2 tablespoons mango chutney
1 cup shredded cooked chicken
1 cup finely shredded red cabbage
1 cup finely shredded romaine lettuce
1/3 cup thinly sliced celery
1/2 cup sliced fresh ripe mango (or canned, drained well)
1/4 cup thinly sliced green onion
1/4 cup sliced almonds, toasted (see page 22 for tips)

Combine the mayonnaise and curry powder in a small bowl. Spread over one half of both tortillas. Spread the other halves with chutney.

Lay the remaining ingredients down the centre of both tortillas and roll up firmly to enclose the filling.

Make ahead: The wraps can be made 3 hours ahead, wrapped in plastic wrap and stored in the fridge.

Makes 2   30 minutes or less

vegetable lentil soup

Keep portions of the soup frozen to take to work for lunch.

1 tablespoon olive oil
2 cups chopped onion (about 2 medium onions)
6 garlic cloves, minced
2 cups chopped carrot (about 3 medium carrots)
1 cup chopped rutabaga (about 1 medium rutabaga)
1 1/2 cups chopped celery (about 6 celery stalks)
1 1/4 cups dried brown lentils
2 quarts (2 litres) vegetable broth
   (your own, see page 19, or store bought)
1 rosemary sprig
2 bay leaves
salt and freshly ground pepper
2 tablespoons lemon juice

Heat the oil in a large pot or Dutch oven over medium-high heat. Add the onion and garlic and cook, stirring occasionally, for about 5 minutes or until the onion is softened.

Add the carrot, rutabaga, celery, lentils, broth, rosemary, bay leaves and a pinch of salt and pepper and stir. Bring to a boil and then reduce the heat to medium-low. Cook, covered, stirring occasionally, for about 40 minutes or until the lentils and vegetables are tender.

Stir in the juice. Remove and discard the rosemary stem and bay leaves before serving. Serve the soup hot.

Make ahead: The soup can be made 3 days ahead and stored in an airtight container in the fridge. Or freeze in airtight containers for up to 6 months.

Serves 6   ✱ make ahead

roasted butternut squash soup

This is a thick soup with a velvety-smooth texture. Add a little more broth if you prefer the soup not as thick. I love it served with lightly buttered, warm multi-grain rolls.

1 tablespoon olive oil
2 cups chopped onion (about 2 medium onions)
6 garlic cloves, minced
1 1/2 teaspoons ground cumin
1 quart (1 litre) chicken broth
   (your own, see page 15, or store bought)
4 lbs (2kg) butternut squash, peeled, seeded and chopped
2 rosemary sprigs
salt and freshly ground pepper
3 tablespoons sour cream

Heat the oil in a large pot or Dutch oven over medium-high heat. Add the onion and cook, stirring occasionally, for about 5 minutes or until softened.

Add the garlic and cumin and cook for 1 minute or until fragrant. Stir in the broth, squash, rosemary and a generous pinch of salt and pepper. Bring to a boil. Reduce the heat to medium-low. Simmer, covered, for about 20 minutes or until the squash is very tender. Let cool for 10 minutes. Remove the rosemary stems.

Put the squash mixture into a blender in batches and blend until smooth. Return the squash mixture to the same pot. Add the sour cream and stir over medium heat until hot.

Make ahead: The soup can be made 3 days ahead and stored in an airtight container in the fridge. Or freeze in airtight containers for up to 6 months.

Serves 6 to 8   ✱ make ahead

warm potato salad
with creamy mustard dressing

This potato salad is as good served cold as it is warm, making it perfect to take on picnics and for barbecues and served with barbecue chicken, steak or sausages.

2 lbs (1kg) small new potatoes
1 tablespoon olive oil
1/2 teaspoon salt
freshly ground pepper
1/3 cup thinly sliced green onion
1/3 cup pine nuts, toasted (see page 22 for tips)

creamy mustard dressing
3 tablespoons sour cream
2 tablespoons white wine vinegar
1 tablespoon grainy mustard
1 tablespoon honey
1 garlic clove, minced
salt and freshly ground pepper

Line a baking sheet with parchment paper. Preheat the oven to 400°F (200°C). Toss the potatoes, oil, salt and a pinch of pepper together on the prepared baking sheet and arrange in a single layer. Roast, uncovered, in the preheated oven, stirring once, for about 35 minutes or until golden and tender. Put the potatoes into a large bowl and add the remaining ingredients.

To make the creamy mustard dressing, whisk all the ingredients in a large bowl. Drizzle over the potato mixture and gently toss. Serve warm or chilled.

Make ahead: The dressing can be made a day ahead and stored in an airtight container in the fridge.

Serves 4

ham and coleslaw sandwich

This sandwich is one of my all-time lunch favourites, especially when served with a steaming hot cup of tea. Use store-bought sweet coleslaw if preferred.

2 tablespoons sour cream
1 tablespoon mayonnaise (your own, see page 21,
   or store bought)
1 tablespoon white wine vinegar
1 teaspoon Dijon mustard
2 teaspoons granulated sugar
salt and freshly ground pepper
1 cup finely chopped savoy cabbage
1/3 cup grated carrot
1/3 cup finely chopped celery
2 tablespoons finely chopped green onion
8 slices multi-grain bread
softened butter for spreading, optional
8 oz (250g) sliced good-quality ham (about 12 slices)

Combine the sour cream, mayonnaise, vinegar, mustard, sugar and a pinch of salt and pepper in a large bowl. Add the cabbage, carrot, celery and green onion and stir until combined.

Spread each slice of the bread with a little butter. Top 4 of the slices with the coleslaw and add the ham; top with the remaining slices.

Make ahead: The coleslaw can be made a day ahead and stored in an airtight container in the fridge. The sandwich is best made just before serving.

Serves 4   ✱ 30 minutes or less

vegetable lentil soup

roasted butternut squash soup

warm potato salad with creamy mustard dressing

ham and coleslaw sandwich

grilled vegetable and goat cheese bruschetta

grilled vegetable and goat cheese bruschetta

This recipe also makes a great appetizer, especially paired with **roasted tomato bruschetta** (page 93). Or serve it for a light lunch.

2 tablespoons balsamic vinegar
2 tablespoons lemon juice
2 tablespoons olive oil, plus 1 teaspoon extra
salt and freshly ground pepper
1 medium zucchini, thinly sliced lengthways
1 small eggplant, thinly sliced lengthways
1 lb (500g) asparagus spears, trimmed of woody ends
8 green onions, trimmed
1 ciabatta loaf or dense multi-grain bread loaf,
  cut into 1/4 inch (6mm) thick slices
2 x 4 1/2 oz (140g) packages goat cheese, softened
3 tablespoons finely chopped fresh basil
1 teaspoon ground cumin

Preheat the barbecue, electric grill or grill pan to medium-high.

Combine the vinegar, juice, 2 tablespoons of oil and a pinch of salt and pepper in a large, shallow dish. Add the zucchini, eggplant, asparagus and green onions and toss until coated.

Grill the vegetables on the preheated barbecue, turning occasionally, for 3 to 4 minutes or until tender and grill marks appear. Finely chop the vegetables and put them into a large bowl.

Brush each slice of bread with the extra oil and grill for about 1 minute on each side or until grill marks appear.

Combine the goat cheese, basil and cumin in a small bowl. Spread onto one side of each slice of warm bread. Top with the vegetable mixture. Serve warm.

Make ahead: The vegetables can be grilled 2 days ahead and stored in an airtight container in the fridge. Let stand at room temperature for 1 hour before serving. The goat cheese mixture can be prepared a day ahead and stored in an airtight container in the fridge. Let stand at room temperature for 1 hour before serving.

Serving suggestion: For a light summer lunch, serve the bruschetta with grilled chicken or pork steaks that have been tossed in lemon juice, olive oil, garlic, basil, salt and freshly ground pepper and then grilled to perfection.

Serves 4   30 minutes or less

steak and onion sandwiches

steak and onion sandwiches

If preferred, you can substitute the tenderloin steaks for fast-fry minute steaks. Or substitute the steak for chicken breast.

1 tablespoon olive oil, plus extra for brushing on steaks
3 cups thinly sliced onion (about 3 medium onions)
1/4 cup orange juice
1 tablespoon red wine vinegar
1 tablespoon packed brown sugar
salt and freshly ground pepper
4 beef tenderloin steaks (about 1 lb/500g)
1 ciabatta loaf or dense multi-grain bread
4 slices Swiss cheese

Heat 1 tablespoon of the oil in a large frying pan over medium-high heat. Add the onion and cook, stirring occasionally, for about 10 minutes or until softened.

Add the juice, vinegar, sugar and a pinch of salt and pepper. Cook, stirring occasionally, until the liquid is evaporated. Cover and keep warm.

Preheat the barbecue, electric grill or grill pan to medium-high.

Place the steaks between 2 pieces of plastic wrap. Pound with the smooth side of a meat mallet or a rolling pin until 1/4 inch (6mm) thickness. Brush each steak with a little of the extra oil and sprinkle with salt and pepper.

Cook the steaks on the preheated barbecue for 2 to 3 minutes on each side or until tender and cooked to your liking.

Cut 8, 1/2 inch (1cm) thick slices from the loaf. Toast on the preheated barbecue for about 1 minute on each side or until golden and grill marks appear. Top 4 slices of bread with a slice of Swiss cheese. Add the steaks and onion mixture and top with the remaining slices. Serve hot.

Make ahead: The sandwiches are best made just before serving.

Serving suggestion: Serve with coleslaw or the **garden salad with blue cheese and maple dressing** (page 63) and corn on the cob.

Serves 4   30 minutes or less

mushroom panini

corned beef and mustard mayonnaise baguette

mushroom panini

A panini is Italian for "small bread". This recipe is for a grilled sandwich using foccacia bread filled with garlic, mushrooms, peppers and melted cheese. You can add almost any filling; the addition of sliced roasted chicken, beef or turkey would be delicious.

1 tablespoon olive oil, plus extra for brushing on bread
2 cups thinly sliced red onion (about 2 medium onions)
2 cups thinly sliced green pepper
    (about 2 medium peppers)
4 cups sliced mushrooms (about 11 oz/340g)
4 garlic cloves, minced
1 tablespoon balsamic vinegar
3 tablespoons chopped fresh parsley
2 tablespoons sour cream
salt and freshly ground pepper
2 foccacia bread loaves, halved horizontally
1 cup grated smoked cheese (such as applewood)

Heat 1 tablespoon of the oil in a large frying pan over medium-high heat. Add the onion and pepper and cook, stirring occasionally, for about 5 minutes or until softened.

Add the mushrooms and garlic and cook, stirring occasionally, for 3 to 5 minutes or until the mushrooms are softened. Add the vinegar and stir until well combined.

Add the parsley, sour cream and a pinch of salt and pepper and stir until combined.

Preheat a large frying pan or grill pan over medium heat.

Sprinkle one half of the cut side of each foccacia with cheddar cheese. Add the mushroom mixture and top with the other foccacia halves. Brush the tops with a little extra oil and place, oiled side down, into the preheated pan.

Cook, pressing the foccacia down with a large egg lifter, for 2 to 3 minutes or until golden. Brush with a little more extra oil before turning. Turn and cook, pressing down with a large egg lifter, for 2 to 3 minutes or until golden and the cheese is melted. Cut each panini into 4 pieces to serve. Serve hot.

Make ahead: The panini is best made just before serving.

Serving suggestion: Serve with **roasted butternut squash soup** (page 52) or **warm tomato and bean salad** (page 68).

Serves 4   30 minutes or less

corned beef and mustard mayonnaise baguette

I love my mum's leftover corned beef sliced up on sandwiches and slathered in hot mustard. Choose to make your own corned beef or buy it sliced from the deli in most grocery stores.

2 tablespoons mayonnaise
    (your own, see page 21, or store bought)
2 teaspoons hot English mustard
1 baguette (20 inch/50cm long), cut crossways
    into quarters and split in half 3/4 of the way through
8 oz (250g) sliced corned beef (about 12 slices)
2 medium ripe tomatoes, sliced
1/4 cup thinly sliced red onion
romaine lettuce leaves
salt and freshly ground pepper

Combine the mayonnaise and mustard in a small bowl. Spread onto the cut sides of each quarter of the baguette.

Fill with the remaining ingredients.

Make ahead: The baguette is best made just before serving. The mayonnaise and mustard mixture can be made a day ahead and stored in an airtight container in the fridge.

Serves 4   30 minutes or less

bacon and egg salad with parmesan dressing

bacon and egg salad
with parmesan dressing

I like to use crusty, Italian-style bread, such as ciabatta or a dense multi-grain variety, in this recipe.

parmesan dressing
3 tablespoons lemon juice
2 tablespoons olive oil
2 tablespoons sour cream
1/4 cup finely grated, fresh parmesan cheese
1 garlic clove, minced
1/2 teaspoon granulated sugar
freshly ground pepper

bacon and egg salad
2 cups cubed bread (1/2 inch/1cm)
2 teaspoons olive oil
1/2 teaspoon paprika
1/2 cup finely chopped back bacon
4 eggs
1 medium romaine lettuce, torn

To make the parmesan dressing, put all the ingredients into a blender and blend until smooth (or use an immersion blender).

To make the bacon and egg salad, grease a baking sheet. Preheat the oven to 375°F (190°C).

Toss the bread, oil, paprika and bacon together on the prepared baking sheet and arrange in a single layer. Toast in the preheated oven, stirring once, for about 10 minutes or until the bread is golden and crisp.

Put the eggs in small saucepan and cover with water. Bring to a gentle boil and cook, uncovered, for 5 minutes. Place the eggs in a bowl of cold water and let stand for 5 minutes. Peel and quarter the eggs.

Put the lettuce, eggs and bread mixture in a large bowl. Drizzle with the dressing and gently toss.

Make ahead: The eggs can be cooked a day ahead and stored in an airtight container in the fridge. The dressing can be made a day ahead and stored in an airtight container in the fridge. Add the dressing to the salad just before serving.

Serving suggestion: Serve the salad with store-bought roasted chicken, large grilled shrimp or grilled chicken breasts.

Serves 4   30 minutes or less

garden salad with blue cheese and maple dressing

garden salad with blue cheese and maple dressing

You can add any raw, fresh vegetable that you fancy to this salad. Sliced cucumber and sugar snap peas make a great addition.

blue cheese and maple dressing

3 tablespoons olive oil
3 tablespoons white wine vinegar
2 1/2 oz (75g) creamy blue cheese
   (such as cambozola), softened
2 tablespoons maple syrup
1 garlic clove, minced (optional)
salt and freshly ground pepper

garden salad

4 cups mixed baby salad leaves
1/2 cup sliced radishes
1/2 cup thinly sliced red onion
1 cup thinly sliced red pepper (about 1 medium pepper)
1 large ripe avocado, thinly sliced
1 cup thinly sliced mushrooms (about 3 1/2 oz/85g)
2 cups cherry (or grape) tomatoes, halved if large
1/2 cup cashews, toasted and coarsely chopped
   (see page 22 for tips)

To make the blue cheese and maple dressing, put all the ingredients into a blender, and blend until smooth (or use an immersion blender).

To make the garden salad, put all the ingredients in a large bowl. Drizzle with the dressing and gently toss.

Make ahead: The dressing can be made a day ahead but omit the garlic. Store in an airtight container in the fridge. The salad is best made just before serving.

Serving suggestion: You can serve this delicious salad with almost anything, although it is especially good with barbecued beef, lamb chops and shrimp.

Serves 4   30 minutes or less

chicken noodle salad
with sesame lime dressing

Cook your own chicken if you have the time, but I find the roasted chickens you buy from the grocery store to be a quick, easy and inexpensive alternative.

sesame lime dressing
1/3 cup lime juice
3 tablespoons peanut oil
3 tablespoons rice vinegar
2 tablespoons fish sauce
1 tablespoon sesame oil
1 tablespoon packed brown sugar

chicken noodle salad
9 1/2 oz (300g) package dried egg noodles
4 cups chopped cooked chicken
   (about 1 store-bought roasted chicken)
2 medium ripe mangoes, sliced (14 oz/398ml can, drained)
6 oz (185g) snow peas, trimmed and thinly sliced
1 1/2 cups bean sprouts
2 cups thinly sliced red pepper (about 2 medium peppers)
1 bunch green onions, thinly sliced
1/3 cup cilantro (coriander) leaves
2 tablespoons sesame seeds, toasted (see page 22 for tips)

To make the sesame lime dressing, put all the ingredients in a jar and shake until well combined.

To make the chicken noodle salad, cook the noodles according to the package directions. Rinse them under cold water and drain well. Put the noodles into a large bowl.

Add the remaining ingredients. Drizzle with the dressing and gently toss. Serve cold.

Make ahead: The dressing can be made a day ahead and stored in an airtight container in the fridge. Add to the salad just before serving.

Serving suggestion: The salad can be served on its own as a meal or as a side salad.

Serves 6 to 8

chicken noodle salad with sesame lime dressing

Choose red, juicy-ripe tomatoes for the best flavour. This delicious soup makes a perfect appetizer for entertaining.

20 Roma (egg) tomatoes (about 3 lbs/1.5kg),
  cored and halved lengthways
2 medium onions, cut into thin wedges
6 garlic cloves, chopped
1 tablespoon olive oil, plus 2 teaspoons extra
salt and freshly ground pepper
1 lb (500g) medium raw shrimp
  (about 3/4 lb/375g peeled weight)
1 cup dry white wine
2 1/2 cups chicken broth
  (your own, see page 15, or store bought)
1/2 cup whipping cream
3 tablespoons Thai sweet chili sauce

Line a large baking sheet with parchment paper. Preheat the oven to 375°F (190°C).

Combine the tomatoes, onions, garlic, 1 tablespoon of oil and a generous pinch of salt and pepper on the prepared baking sheet. Roast, uncovered, in the preheated oven for about 40 minutes or until the tomatoes are softened.

Peel and devein the shrimp, reserving their shells. Coarsely chop the shrimp and set aside in an airtight container in the fridge until ready to use.

Heat the extra oil in a medium saucepan over medium-high heat. Add the shrimp shells and cook, stirring occasionally, for 3 minutes. Stir in the wine and boil, uncovered, for about 3 minutes or until the wine is reduced by about half. Add the broth and bring to a boil. Reduce the heat to low, cover and simmer for 5 minutes to infuse the flavours. Strain the broth mixture through a fine seive into a large bowl. Discard the shells. Stir in the tomato mixture.

Put the combined tomato and broth mixture into a blender in batches and blend until smooth. Pour into a large saucepan and bring to a gentle boil over medium-high heat. Add the cream, sauce and reserved shrimp and stir for about 2 minutes or until the shrimp are just tender; do not overcook.

Make ahead: The tomato soup base can be made a day ahead and stored in an airtight container in the fridge. Heat the soup base over medium-high heat before adding the shrimp.

Serving suggestion: Serve with crusty, Italian-style or multi-grain bread.

Serves 6 to 8   ❋ make ahead

roasted tomato and shrimp soup

warm tomato and bean salad

Use navy or white kidney beans in this salad and adjust the chili to suit your taste.

1 1/2 tablespoons olive oil
3 cups cherry (or grape) tomatoes, halved if large
4 garlic cloves, thinly sliced
1 teaspoon sambal oelek (chili paste)
2 teaspoons balsamic vinegar
2 teaspoons Thai sweet chili sauce
2 cups cooked white kidney beans (your own, see page 16, or 19 oz/540ml can, rinsed and drained)
2 tablespoons lemon juice
2 tablespoons finely shredded fresh basil
salt and freshly ground pepper

Heat the oil in a large frying pan over high heat. Add the tomatoes and garlic and cook, stirring occasionally, for about 5 minutes or until the tomatoes are wilted.

Add the remaining ingredients and gently stir until combined and warm. Serve warm.

Make ahead: The salad is best made just before serving, but it is also delicious served cold. If you do serve it cold, it can be made a day ahead.

Serving suggestion: Serve with barbecued lamb chops, steaks or chicken and grilled broccoli florets. This salad is also delicious tossed through hot cooked spaghetti.

Serves 4 to 6   30 minutes or less   make ahead

warm tomato and bean salad

tuna pasta salad with dill dressing

tuna pasta salad with dill dressing

Sun-dried olives are available in some grocery stores and specialty food stores. If they are not available, use black olives of your choice.

dill dressing

1/4 cup mayonnaise (your own, see page 21,
  or store bought)
3 tablespoons red wine vinegar
3 tablespoons chopped fresh dill
1 garlic clove, minced
salt and freshly ground pepper

tuna pasta salad

4 cups medium fusili pasta
6 oz (170ml) jar artichokes, drained and coarsely chopped
12 cherry (or grape) tomatoes, halved if large
1 cup roasted red peppers
  (your own, see page 10, or store bought)
1/3 cup sun-dried black olives (or olives of your choice)
1/4 cup thinly sliced red onion
2 x 6 oz (170g) cans flaked white tuna, drained

To make the dill dressing, whisk all the ingredients in a small bowl until well combined.

To make the tuna pasta salad, cook the pasta in boiling salted water in a large pot or Dutch oven, stirring occasionally, for about 12 minutes or until al dente. Drain and rinse under cold water; drain well.

Put the pasta and the remaining ingredients in a large bowl. Drizzle with the dressing and gently toss.

Make ahead: The salad can be prepared the night before and stored in an airtight container in the fridge. The dressing can be made the night before and stored in an airtight container in the fridge. Add the dressing to the salad just before serving.

Serving suggestion: Serve this salad as a meal with barbecued meat and an arugula or spinach salad or just have it on its own.

Serves 4 to 6   30 minutes or less   make ahead

appetizers

Open the wine, gather friends and family around.
Enjoy good times with fuss-free appetizers that
are made ahead or whipped up in no time flat.
Relax and spend time with your guests.

A light, fresh lemon grass broth is the perfect base for tender mint-flavoured dumplings. You can buy lemon grass in grocery stores and in Asian markets.

dumplings

2 skinless, boneless chicken breasts, cut into pieces
11 oz (345g) medium raw shrimp, peeled and deveined
　　(about 8 oz/250g peeled weight)
2 tablespoons chopped fresh mint
2 tablespoons hoisin sauce
2 garlic cloves, chopped
1 egg
1/2 teaspoon freshly ground pepper

lemon grass broth

2 quarts (2 litres) chicken broth
　　(your own, see page 15, or store bought)
2 lemon grass stalks, trimmed and each cut into 3 pieces
1 tablespoon hoisin sauce
1 tablespoon finely grated ginger
1/3 cup thinly sliced green onion
salt

To make the dumplings, put all the ingredients into a food processor and process until finely chopped and well combined.

To make the lemon grass broth, combine the broth, lemon grass, sauce and ginger in a large pot or Dutch oven. Cover and bring to a boil. Reduce the heat to medium-low. Simmer for 15 minutes for the flavours to infuse.

Remove and discard the lemon grass and increase the heat to medium-high.

Working quickly, drop heaped tablespoons of the dumpling mixture into the simmering broth mixture (the dumplings won't be perfectly round). Cook for about 5 minutes or until the dumplings are cooked through.

Stir in the green onion and a pinch of salt. Serve hot.

Make ahead: The broth mixture and dumpling mixture can be prepared a day ahead and stored separately in airtight containers in the fridge. Bring the broth to a simmer before cooking the dumplings in it.

Serves 8 　　　　　　　　　　　　　　　✳ make ahead

shrimp and chicken dumpling soup

corn cakes with avocado salsa

corn cakes with avocado salsa

Serve these corn cakes stacked on individual plates or put them on a large platter, top each one with a little dollop of sour cream and add some of the salsa.

avocado salsa

2 medium ripe avocados, diced
2 tablespoons lime juice
2 tablespoons chopped fresh cilantro (coriander)
salt and freshly ground pepper

corn cakes

2 teaspoons olive oil, plus 2 tablespoons extra
1/2 cup finely chopped red onion
1/2 cup finely chopped red pepper
2 garlic cloves, minced
1 cup all-purpose flour
2 teaspoons baking powder
1 teaspoons ground cumin
1 1/2 cups corn kernels (or 14 oz/398ml can, drained)
1/4 cup grated white cheddar cheese
salt and freshly ground pepper
3 eggs
2/3 cup buttermilk

To make the avocado salsa, combine all the ingredients in a small bowl.

To make the corn cakes, heat 2 teaspoons of the oil in a large frying pan, preferably non-stick, over medium heat. Add the onion, red pepper and garlic and cook, stirring occasionally, for about 5 minutes or until softened.

Combine the flour, baking powder and cumin into a medium bowl. Add the corn, cheddar cheese, onion mixture and a pinch of salt and pepper and stir until well combined.

Whisk the eggs and buttermilk in a small bowl. Add to the flour mixture and stir until well combined.

Heat some of the extra oil in the same frying pan (which has been wiped clean) over medium heat. Drop 2 tablespoons of the mixture into the pan, about 2 inches (5cm) apart, and spread to make a 2 inch (5cm) pancake. Repeat with remaining mixture (you will need to cook these in 2 or 3 batches). Cook for 2 to 3 minutes on each side or until golden and cooked through. Place on a plate and cover with foil to keep warm. Serve with the **avocado salsa**.

Make ahead: The corn cakes and salsa are best made just before serving.

Serving suggestion: Serve with sour cream.

Serves 6

fish cakes with mango lime sauce

Red curry paste, rice vermicelli noodles and fish sauce are available in the Asian section of most grocery stores or in Asian markets. You will need about 2 ripe mangoes for this recipe, or if fresh mangoes are not available, use drained canned ones instead.

mango lime sauce
1/4 cup lime juice
2 tablespoons Thai sweet chili sauce
2 tablespoons water
1 teaspoon fish sauce
3/4 cup finely chopped ripe mango
    (or about 1/2 x 14 oz/398ml can, drained)
2 tablespoons finely chopped red onion

fish cakes
2 oz (60g) rice vermicelli noodles
1 ripe mango, finely chopped
    (or 1/2 x 14 oz/398ml can drained)
3/4 lb (375g) snapper fillets
11 oz (345g) medium raw shrimp, peeled and deveined
    (about 8 oz/250g peeled weight)
2 tablespoons coarsely chopped fresh cilantro (coriander)
1 tablespoon Thai red curry paste
2 garlic cloves, chopped
2 teaspoons finely grated ginger
2 teaspoons fish sauce
1 egg
1 tablespoon peanut oil

To make the mango lime sauce, combine all the ingredients in a small saucepan and stir over medium heat until warm. Remove from the heat; cover and keep warm.

To make the fish cakes, put the noodles in a medium heatproof bowl and cover with boiling water. Let stand for about 10 minutes or until softened; drain well. Coarsely chop the noodles and place them in a large bowl. Stir in the mango and set aside.

Place the snapper and shrimp on paper towel to absorb any excess moisture. Put the cilantro, curry paste, garlic, ginger, sauce, egg, snapper and shrimp into a food processor and process until finely chopped.

Add the shrimp mixture to the noodle mixture and stir until well combined.

Shape 2 tablespoons of the mixture into a patty shape. Repeat with the remaining mixture. Heat a little of the oil in a large frying pan, preferable non-stick, over medium heat. Cook the fish cakes in 3 batches for 2 to 3 minutes on each side, or until golden brown and cooked. Place on a plate and cover with foil to keep warm while cooking the remaining fish cakes. Serve warm with the **mango lime sauce.**

Make ahead: The fish cakes can be prepared a day ahead and stored, covered, in the fridge. Cook them just before serving. The sauce is best made just before serving.

Serves 4 to 6   make ahead

fish cakes with mango lime sauce

thai-style beef lettuce wraps

thai-style beef lettuce wraps

For those of you who can't eat peanuts, simply omit them from the recipe.

1/2 cup thinly sliced red onion
1/4 cup lime juice
2 butter lettuce
1 1/2 lbs (750g) ground beef
4 garlic cloves, minced
2 teaspoons finely grated ginger
3 tablespoons chopped fresh mint
3 tablespoons chopped fresh cilantro (coriander)
3 tablespoons Thai sweet chili sauce
1 tablespoon hoisin sauce
1 tablespoon fish sauce
3/4 cup coarsely grated carrot
1/3 cup peanuts, toasted (see page 22 for tips)

Combine the onion and juice in a small bowl and let stand for 15 minutes. (This will help to mellow the flavour of the onion.)

Separate the leaves from both lettuce and set aside the large and very small leaves for another use. You need about 24 of the small to medium leaves.

Heat a large frying pan, preferably non-stick, over medium-high heat. Add the beef and cook, breaking up any lumps, for about 10 minutes or until browned. (It is important to the flavour of the dish to brown the meat well.) Drain any fat from the pan.

Add the garlic and ginger and cook for about 1 minute or until fragrant.

Remove the pan from the heat and add the onion mixture, mint, cilantro, sauces and carrot and stir until well combined. Or, as an option, top with carrots just before serving.

Spoon the mixture (about 2 heaped tablespoons) into each lettuce leaf and sprinkle with the peanuts.

Make ahead: The wraps are best made just before serving.

Serving suggestion: There are two ways to serve this dish: you can put the beef mixture into a bowl and place the lettuce leaves around the bowl and let people help themselves or you can assemble them as above.

Serves 6   30 minutes or less

white bean and roasted garlic dip

garlic shrimp on toast

asian nut mix

asparagus soup

white bean and roasted garlic dip

When garlic is roasted it's transformed into a buttery smooth texture and its flavour mellows, so don't be shocked by all the garlic in this dip. For the white beans, you can use navy or white kidney beans.

2 garlic bulbs
3 tablespoons olive oil
4 cups cooked white beans (your own, see page 16,
    or 2 x 19 oz/540ml cans, rinsed and drained)
1/3 cup lemon juice
2 tablespoons sour cream
salt and freshly ground pepper
ground paprika, sprinkle

Preheat the oven to 350°F (180°C). Remove and discard the excess paper coating from both garlic bulbs. Wrap the garlic bulbs individually in foil and place on a baking sheet. Cook in the preheated oven for about 40 minutes or until softened. Open the foil and let stand for about 10 minutes or until the garlic bulbs are cool enough to handle.

Squeeze the garlic from each clove into a food processor. Add the oil, beans, juice, sour cream and a pinch of salt and pepper and process until smooth. Scrape the mixture into a serving bowl. Sprinkle with paprika. Serve warm or at room temperature.

Make ahead: The dip can be made a day ahead and stored in an airtight container in the fridge. Let it come to room temperature before serving.

Serving suggestion: Serve with toasted pita bread, celery sticks, baby carrots and radishes.

Makes about 3 1/2 cups   30 minutes or less   make ahead

asian nut mix

You can line the baking sheet with parchment paper for easier clean-up, but I found it difficult to toss the nuts. Using a large baking sheet allows the mixture to spread out and crisp up nicely.

2 tablespoons honey
1 tablespoon soy sauce
1 tablespoon hoisin sauce
1/2 teaspoon freshly ground pepper
1/4 teaspoon five-spice powder
1 cup natural almonds
1 cup pecans
1 cup cashew nuts
1 cup macadamia nuts
1 cup pine nuts

Grease a large baking sheet. Preheat the oven to 350°F (180°C).

Combine the honey, sauces, pepper and five-spice powder in a large bowl.

Add the remaining ingredients and stir until the nuts are well coated. Spread the nut mixture onto the prepared baking sheet and cook in the preheated oven, stirring occasionally, for 20 to 25 minutes or until golden brown (the nut mix will become crisp as it cools). Cool completely before storing.

Make ahead: The nut mix can be made 2 weeks ahead and stored in an airtight container in a cool, dry place. Do not store in the fridge because the nuts may become sticky.

Makes about 5 cups   make ahead

garlic shrimp on toast

Choose crusty, dense baguettes: The nicer the bread, the better these will be.

12 inch (30cm) baguette, cut diagonally
    into 24 x 1/2 inch (1cm) slices
1 tablespoon olive oil
1 tablespoon butter
4 garlic cloves, minced
2 medium ripe tomatoes, finely chopped
2 tablespoons chopped fresh basil
1/2 teaspoon sambal oelek (chili paste)
salt and freshly ground pepper
1 lb (500g) medium raw shrimp, peeled, deveined
    and coarsely chopped (about 3/4 lb/375g peeled weight)
3/4 cup finely grated, fresh parmesan cheese

Preheat the oven to 375°F (190°C). Place the bread slices in a single layer on a large baking sheet. Toast in the preheated oven for 10 to 12 minutes or until lightly golden; set aside on the baking sheet.

Heat the oil, butter and garlic in a large frying pan over low heat. Cook, stirring occasionally, for about 3 minutes or until the garlic is softened and fragrant. Add the tomatoes, basil, sambal oelek and a pinch of salt and pepper. Cook, stirring occasionally, for about 3 minutes or until the tomatoes are softened. Increase the heat to medium-high.

Stir in the shrimp and cook, stirring constantly, for 2 to 3 minutes or until the shrimp are just cooked; do not overcook. Top each toast with the shrimp mixture. Sprinkle with the parmesan cheese and place under a hot broiler for about 1 minute or until the cheese is melted.

Make ahead: These are best made just before serving.

Serves 4 to 6   30 minutes or less

asparagus soup

Make sure you give the leek a good rinse to remove any dirt that can get trapped between the layers.

1 tablespoon olive oil
1 leek, white and tender green parts only, sliced
6 large shallots (eshallots), sliced
1 tablespoon butter
2 tablespoons all-purpose flour
1 cup dry white wine
2 cups milk
2 cups chicken broth (your own, see page 15, or store bought)
2 lbs (1kg) asparagus, trimmed of woody ends,
    cut into 1 inch (2.5cm) pieces
salt and freshly ground pepper

Heat the oil in a large saucepan over medium heat. Add the leek and shallots and cook, stirring occasionally, for about 10 minutes or until softened.

Add the butter and stir until melted. Add the flour and cook, stirring constantly, for 1 minute. Gradually stir in the wine, milk and broth. Bring to a boil and add the asparagus and a pinch of salt and pepper. Cook, uncovered, for about 20 minutes or until the asparagus is softened.

Put the asparagus mixture in a blender in batches and blend until smooth and frothy. Return the mixture to the same pan and stir over medium heat until hot. Serve hot.

Make ahead: This soup is best made on the day of serving.

Serves 4 to 6   30 minutes or less

mussels in white wine, basil and chili

When buying mussels, look for ones that are closed, or ones that close when you touch them, which means that they are still alive. If you aren't using them on the day of purchase, place them in a glass bowl, cover them with a damp, clean tea towel and store in the fridge. Sambal oelek (chili paste) is available in grocery stores and in Asian markets.

1 tablespoon butter
2/3 cup finely chopped onion
4 garlic cloves, minced
1 cup dry white wine
1 teaspoon sambal oelek (chili paste)
1/2 cup whipping cream
3 lbs (1.5kg) mussels, cleaned and beards removed
3 tablespoons chopped fresh basil
salt and freshly ground pepper

Melt the butter in a wok or large deep frying pan over medium heat. Add the onion and garlic and cook, stirring occasionally, for about 10 minutes or until the onion is softened.

Stir in the wine and sambal oelek and boil gently, uncovered, for about 3 minutes or until the mixture has reduced by half.

Stir in the cream and reduce the heat to medium.

Add the mussels and stir. Cook, covered, stirring occasionally, for about 3 minutes or until the mussels are opened and tender. Do not overcook; discard any unopened mussels.

Stir in the basil and a pinch of salt and pepper.
Serve immediately.

Make ahead: The mussels can be cleaned and stored in the fridge a day ahead. Cook the mussels just before serving.

Serving suggestion: Serve with crusty bread for soaking up the leftover sauce. To make a meal, serve with a tossed garden salad.

Serves 4 to 6   30 minutes or less

mussels in white wine, basil and chili

roasted butternut squash salad

roasted butternut squash salad

This is one of my favourite salad recipes—it looks pretty, it has a wonderful flavour and it is incredibly versatile. I like to serve it as an appetizer, as a side salad or as part of a main meal. Anyway you serve it, I am sure it will become a favourite of yours, too.

maple dressing
2 tablespoons olive oil
2 tablespoons white wine vinegar
2 tablespoons maple syrup
2 teaspoons Dijon mustard
salt and freshly ground pepper

roasted butternut squash salad
2 1/2 lbs (1.25kg) butternut squash
3 tablespoons Thai sweet chili sauce
2 teaspoons olive oil
2 rosemary sprigs
1 medium red onion, cut into thin wedges
salt and freshly ground pepper
6 cups mixed baby lettuce leaves
4 oz (125g) goat cheese, crumbled
1/3 cup sliced almonds, toasted (see page 22 for tips)

To make the maple dressing, put all the ingredients in a jar and shake until well combined.

To make the roasted butternut squash salad, line a large baking sheet with parchment paper. Preheat the oven to 400°F (200°C).

Peel the squash, cut in half lengthways, and scrape out and discard the seeds. Cut into 1/4 inch (6mm) thick slices.

Combine the squash, sauce, oil, rosemary, onion and a pinch of salt and pepper on the prepared baking sheet and arrange in a single layer. Roast, uncovered, in the preheated oven, turning once during cooking, for 30 to 40 minutes or until tender and golden. Remove the rosemary stems.

Put the lettuce, goat cheese, almonds and squash mixture in a large bowl. Drizzle with the dressing and toss gently.

Make ahead: The dressing can be made a day ahead and stored in a jar in the fridge. Remove from the fridge 1 hour before serving.

Serves 6

scallop salad with mint vinaigrette

The crisp wontons add a nice crunch to the salad, but it's also delicious served without them if you prefer.

crisps
4 egg roll wrappers
   (freeze the remaining wrappers for another use)
olive oil for brushing

mint vinaigrette
2 tablespoons olive oil
2 tablespoons white wine vinegar
2 tablespoons chopped fresh mint
1 teaspoon honey
salt and freshly ground pepper

scallop salad
12 large scallops
salt and freshly ground pepper
2 teaspoons olive oil
1 cup diced apple (about 1 large apple)
4 cups mixed baby lettuce leaves

To make the crisps, preheat the oven to 350°F (180°C). Brush the egg roll wrappers with a little oil and cut each into 4 triangles. Place on a baking sheet, in a single layer and bake in the preheated oven for about 5 minutes or until golden brown. Set aside until cooled.

To make the mint vinaigrette, put all the ingredients in a jar and shake until well combined.

To make the scallop salad, remove and discard the small muscle on the side of each scallop (if it is there). Place the scallops on paper towel to absorb any excess moisture. Sprinkle them with salt and pepper.

Heat the oil in a medium frying pan over medium-high heat. Cook the scallops for about 1 minute on each side, or until lightly browned and just cooked; do not overcook. Place the scallops on a plate and cover them with foil to keep warm.

Cook the apple in the same pan, stirring occasionally, for about 2 minutes or until softened and warm.

To serve, place the lettuce leaves on individual serving plates. Add the scallops and apple and drizzle with the vinaigrette. Place the crisps on the side of each plate. Or, you can make one large salad by tossing all the ingredients, except the crisps, in a serving bowl. Top with the crisps and serve immediately.

Make ahead: The vinaigrette can be made a day ahead and stored in a jar in the fridge. Remove from the fridge 1 hour before serving. The salad is best made just before serving.

Serves 4   30 minutes or less

mushroom and pesto pizza

This pizza uses phyllo pastry as a base. It crisps perfectly, but because this pastry is so delicate don't overload it with ingredients.

1 tablespoon olive oil, plus 2 tablespoons extra
3 cups thinly sliced onion (about 3 medium onions)
6 garlic cloves, minced
2 teaspoons balsamic vinegar
salt and freshly ground pepper
12 sheets phyllo pastry, thawed
3 tablespoons basil pesto
   (your own, see page 21, or store bought)
2 cups thinly sliced mushrooms
   (about 5 1/2 oz/170g mushrooms)
1/2 cup thinly sliced sun-dried tomatoes in oil,
   drained and sliced
1 cup finely grated, fresh parmesan cheese

Heat 1 tablespoon of the oil in a large frying pan over medium-high heat. Add the onion and cook, stirring occasionally, for about 10 minutes or until softened.

Add the garlic and vinegar and stir for 1 minute or until fragrant. Stir in a pinch of salt and pepper; let cool.

Grease a large 10 x 15 inch (25 x 38cm) baking sheet. Preheat the oven to 375°F (190°C).

Line the prepared baking sheet with 1 sheet of pastry; you should have over-hanging pastry. Brush the pastry lightly with some of the extra oil. Layer with another sheet of pastry and brush with a little more oil. Repeat with the remaining pastry and oil. Tuck the over-hanging pastry under to create a rim.

Spread the pesto over the base of the pastry. Scatter the onion mixture, mushrooms and tomatoes over the pesto and sprinkle with the parmesan cheese. Bake in the preheated oven, on the second bottom rack, for about 15 minutes or until the pastry is golden brown. Cut into 12 pieces to serve. Serve hot.

Make ahead: This pizza is best made just before serving. The onion mixture can be prepared a day ahead and stored in an airtight container in the fridge.

Serves 4

scallop salad with mint vinaigrette

mushroom and pesto pizza

pesto meatballs with tomatoes

This dish is a great starter, but if you add some pasta, it makes a perfect main meal served with a salad. If you don't have any fresh breadcrumbs, then use 1 cup of dried breadcrumbs.

1 lb (500g) ground beef
1 cup grated onion (about 2 large onions)
4 garlic cloves, minced
1 1/2 cups fresh breadcrumbs (see page 21 for tips)
3 tablespoons basil pesto
   (your own, see page 21, or store bought)
1/3 cup chopped fresh parsley
1/3 cup pine nuts, toasted (see page 22 for tips)
1/3 cup finely grated, fresh parmesan cheese
1 egg, lightly beaten
salt and freshly ground pepper
2 cups stewed tomatoes (your own, see page 13,
   or store-bought chunky pasta sauce)

Grease a wire rack and place on a baking sheet lined with parchment paper. Preheat the oven to 350°F (180°C).

Combine the beef, onion, garlic, breadcrumbs, pesto, parsley, pine nuts, parmesan cheese, egg and a pinch of salt and pepper in a large bowl until well mixed.

Shape into heaped 1 tablespoon balls. Place on the prepared wire rack and bake in the preheated oven for about 35 minutes or until browned and cooked through.

Heat the stewed tomatoes in a large frying pan over medium-high heat until hot. Add the meatballs and gently stir until they are coated. Serve hot.

Make ahead: The meatballs can be prepared a day ahead and stored, covered, in the fridge. They can be frozen in an airtight container for up to 3 months.

Serves 6 to 8   make ahead

pesto meatballs with tomatoes

roasted tomato bruschetta

roasted tomato bruschetta

The tomatoes take about 4 hours to slowly roast in the oven, so this recipe is best made a day ahead of serving. This recipe is one of my favourite appetizers because it is easy to prepare and can be made days in advance; just make sure you use fresh garlic to prevent it turning green in the vinegar. These tomatoes are one essential that I always have in the fridge, ready to add to salads, pastas and sandwiches or just to snack on, but be warned, they're addictive!

20 medium ripe Roma (egg) tomatoes (3 lbs/1.5kg),
   cored and halved lengthways
3 tablespoons Thai sweet chili sauce
salt and freshly ground pepper
1/4 cup olive oil, plus extra for brushing on bread
2 tablespoons balsamic vinegar
4 garlic cloves, thinly sliced
1 ciabatta loaf or other crusty bread
parmesan cheese shavings

Grease a large wire rack and place it on a baking sheet lined with parchment paper. Preheat the oven to 325°F (160°C).

Place the tomatoes, cut side up, on the prepared rack and brush with the sauce. Sprinkle with a good pinch of salt and pepper.

Roast in the preheated oven for 3 1/2 to 4 hours or until wilted and browned a little around the edges.

Combine 1/4 cup of the oil, vinegar and garlic in a large jar. Add the tomatoes and gently stir to coat; seal the jar. Marinate in the fridge for at least 8 hours or overnight. Remove from the fridge 1 hour before serving. Drain from the marinade just before serving.

Preheat the oven to 375°F (190°C). Cut the bread into 1/4 inch (6 mm) thick slices. Place the bread slices in a single layer on a large baking sheet. Toast in the preheated oven for 10 to 12 minutes or until lightly golden.

Top the toasts with pieces of tomato and parmesan cheese.

Make ahead: The tomatoes can be made 3 weeks ahead and stored in an airtight container in the fridge.

Serving suggestion: Serve with aged cheddar cheese or parmesan cheese shavings.

Serves 6   make ahead

mains

Nourish the body and warm the soul. The smell of a roast wafting through the house or a steak sizzling on the barbecue. Nothing beats the welcome smells of a home-cooked meal. Set the table, light some candles and savour the moment.

roast lamb and vegetables with port sauce

Being an Aussie, I grew up eating lots of lamb, and today it is still my favourite meat. It is sweet and succulent, and I find it can be quite forgiving for those that aren't too familiar with cooking it. If there are any leftovers, slice them up thinly and have them on a sandwich for lunch the next day with some mango chutney—delicious! Lamb can be found fresh and frozen in grocery and specialty food stores.

3 tablespoons Dijon mustard
2 tablespoons chopped fresh thyme
salt and freshly ground pepper
4 lbs (2kg) bone-in lamb leg
4 garlic cloves, quartered
1 tablespoon olive oil
1 lb (500g) sweet potato (yam), peeled and chopped
3 medium carrots, peeled and chopped
3 medium parsnips, peeled and chopped
3 medium onions, peeled and quartered
4 thyme sprigs
4 garlic cloves, bruised (see page 22 for tips)

port sauce
2 tablespoons all-purpose flour
2 cups chicken broth (your own, see page 15, or store bought)
1/2 cup port
1/2 cup red or black currant jelly
salt and freshly ground pepper

Grease a wire rack and place it in a large, shallow roasting pan. Preheat the oven to 350°F (180°C).

Combine the mustard, thyme and a pinch of salt and pepper in a small bowl.

Using a small sharp knife, make 16 small incisions over the lamb and poke a piece of garlic into each one. Rub the lamb all over with the mustard mixture. Place on the prepared wire rack and roast, uncovered, in the preheated oven for 1 1/2 to 2 hours or until cooked to your liking. Reserve any pan drippings. Cover the lamb with foil to keep warm and let stand for 15 minutes before carving.

While the lamb is cooking, line a large baking sheet with parchment paper. Combine the oil, a pinch of salt and pepper and the remaining ingredients on the prepared baking sheet and arrange in a single layer. Roast, uncovered, in the oven with the lamb, turning occasionally, for about 1 hour or until the vegetables are browned and tender.

To make the port sauce, heat the reserved pan drippings in the same roasting pan over medium heat until hot. Add the flour and cook, stirring constantly, for 1 minute. Whisk in the remaining ingredients. Bring to a boil and boil gently, uncovered, stirring occasionally, for 5 to 10 minutes or until thickened.

Serve the sliced lamb with the roasted vegetables and the sauce.

Make ahead: The lamb, vegetables and sauce are best made just before serving.

Serving suggestion: Serve with steamed fresh or frozen peas.

Serves 6

roast lamb and vegetables with port sauce

peppered buffalo steak
with roasted corn salsa

If buffalo is unavailable, use beef tenderloin or rib eye steaks instead. If corn on the cob is unavailable, use frozen corn and cook it in a grill pan or frying pan.

roasted corn salsa
2 corn cobs (or 2 cups frozen corn kernels, thawed)
1 teaspoon olive oil
2 tablespoons lime juice
2 tablespoons chopped fresh cilantro (coriander)
1 teaspoon packed brown sugar
1 jalapeño pepper, seeded and finely chopped
1/2 teaspoon ground cumin
salt and freshly ground pepper
2 medium ripe tomatoes, quartered, seeded and chopped

peppered buffalo steak
4 buffalo tenderloin steaks (about 1 lb/500g)
1 teaspoon olive oil
2 tablespoons coarsely ground fresh pepper
4 garlic cloves, minced
salt

To make the roasted corn salsa, preheat a barbecue or grill pan to medium-high and then grease. Remove and discard the husks and silk from the corn. Brush with the oil and place on the preheated grill. Cook, turning occasionally, for 5 to 7 minutes or until the corn is cooked and a little charred. Remove from the heat and let stand for about 5 minutes or until cool enough to handle.

Stand one corn cob on its end in a medium, shallow dish and run a knife down the length of the cob to remove the kernels. Repeat with the remaining cob.

Whisk the juice, cilantro, sugar, jalapeño, cumin and a pinch of salt and pepper in a medium bowl until combined.

Add the corn and tomatoes and stir until combined.

To make the peppered buffalo steaks, brush both sides of each steak with the oil. Press the pepper and garlic into the steaks and sprinkle with a pinch of salt.

Preheat a barbecue or grill pan to medium-high and then grease. Cook the steaks on the preheated grill for about 3 minutes on each side, depending on the thickness of the steaks, or until cooked to your liking (buffalo is a lean meat, so it is best cooked to rare or medium-rare). Remove the steaks from the heat and cover with foil to keep warm for 10 minutes before serving.

Serve the steaks with the salsa.

Make ahead: The salsa can be made a day ahead and stored in an airtight container in the fridge, although it is best made just before serving.

Serving suggestion: Serve with a salad of mixed lettuce leaves, thinly sliced green peppers, green onion and chopped avocado; drizzle with some lime juice and olive oil.

Serves 4   30 minutes or less

peppered buffalo steak with roasted corn salsa

balsamic chicken with herb garlic potatoes

balsamic chicken
with herb garlic potatoes

Chicken thighs can be used in place of the drumsticks. If using chicken thighs, reduce the cooking time by about 15 minutes.

1/4 cup balsamic vinegar
1 tablespoon finely grated lemon zest
3 tablespoons lemon juice
2 tablespoons olive oil
2 tablespoons Dijon mustard
salt and freshly ground pepper to taste
12 chicken drumsticks, skin removed*

herb garlic potatoes
2 lbs (1kg) small baby potatoes
3 tablespoons chopped fresh oregano
1 tablespoon olive oil
1/2 teaspoon crushed dried chilies
3 garlic cloves, minced
salt and freshly ground pepper
2 tablespoons lemon juice

Combine the vinegar, zest, juice, oil, mustard and a pinch of salt and pepper in a large, shallow baking dish or a resealable plastic bag. Add the chicken and mix to combine. Cover or seal and marinate in the fridge for 3 hours or overnight.

Grease a large, shallow baking dish. Preheat the oven to 375°F (190°C).

Add the chicken and any marinade to the prepared dish and cover with foil. Roast in the preheated oven for 45 minutes. Remove the foil, turn the chicken and roast, uncovered, a further 30 minutes or until tender and cooked through.

To make the herb garlic potatoes, line a large baking sheet with parchment paper. Combine the potatoes, oregano, oil, chili, garlic and a pinch of salt and pepper on the prepared baking sheet; arrange in a single layer. Roast, uncovered, in the oven with the chicken, turning occasionally, for about 1 hour or until the potatoes are golden and tender.

Drizzle with the juice and stir. Serve hot with the chicken.

Make ahead: The chicken can be marinated a day ahead and stored in an airtight container in the fridge. The potatoes are best made just before serving.

Serving suggestion: Serve with steamed green beans or lightly sautéed spinach and garlic.

* To remove the skin from the chicken drumsticks (or thighs), moisten your fingers and coat them liberally in salt. Pull the skin back towards the knuckle end, using more salt if needed to help you grip the skin.

Serves 6

pan-fried fish
with citrus almond butter

Try including more fish in your diet; it is quick to cook and good for you.

citrus almond butter
2 teaspoons butter
2 teaspoons olive oil
1/4 cup sliced almonds
3 tablespoons orange juice
1 tablespoon lemon juice
1/2 teaspoon finely grated orange zest
2 tablespoons chopped fresh chives
salt and freshly ground pepper

pan-fried fish
1 1/2 lbs (750g) firm white fish fillets
    (such as snapper or halibut), cut into 8 pieces
all-purpose flour
2 eggs, lightly beaten
2 cups finely grated, fresh parmesan cheese
1 tablespoon olive oil, approximately

To make the citrus almond butter, heat the butter and oil in a small frying pan over medium heat until the butter is melted. Add the almonds and cook, stirring constantly, for about 3 minutes or until they are golden. Add the remaining ingredients and stir until hot.

To make the pan-fried fish, coat the fish in flour and shake off the excess. Dip the fish in the egg and sprinkle it with the parmesan cheese, pressing the cheese lightly into the fish.

Heat the oil in a large frying pan, preferably non-stick, over medium heat. Cook the fish in batches for 2 to 3 minutes on each side or until golden and just cooked; do not overcook.

Drizzle the butter over the fish. Serve hot.

Make ahead: The fish is best made just before serving.

Serving suggestion: Serve with steamed baby potatoes and steamed green beans.

Serves 4   30 minutes or less

---

red pepper, chicken
and bean quesadillas

Jalapeño spread or jelly is available in grocery and specialty food stores.

1 tablespoon olive oil, plus 1 teaspoon extra
2 cups thinly sliced onion (about 2 medium onions)
1 cup thinly sliced red pepper (about 1 medium pepper)
2 garlic cloves, minced
1 tablespoon ground chili powder
2 teaspoons ground cumin
1 lb (500g) ground chicken
2 medium ripe tomatoes, chopped
1/3 cup chopped fresh cilantro (coriander)
3 tablespoons jalapeño spread (or jelly)
salt and freshly ground pepper
6 large whole-wheat tortillas
14 oz (398ml) can refried beans
1 1/2 cups grated jalapeño jack cheese

Heat 1 tablespoon of the oil in a large frying pan over medium-high heat. Add the onion and red pepper and cook, stirring occasionally, for about 10 minutes or until the onion is softened and lightly browned.

Add the garlic, chili powder and cumin and cook, stirring constantly, for about 1 minute or until fragrant.

Add the chicken, tomatoes, cilantro, jalapeño spread and salt and pepper and cook, stirring occasionally and breaking up any large pieces of chicken, for about 10 minutes or until the chicken is browned and the sauce is thickened.

Place the tortillas in a single layer on a smooth surface. Spread each tortilla with the refried beans. Top one half of each tortilla with the chicken mixture and then sprinkle with the jalapeno cheese. Fold the other half of the tortilla over and press down lightly to seal. Brush with the extra oil.

Preheat a grill pan or large frying pan, preferably non-stick, over medium heat. Cook the quesadillas in the preheated pan for about 3 minutes on each side or until golden and crisp.

Make ahead: The chicken filling can be made a day ahead and reheated before adding it to the quesadilla.

Serving suggestion: Serve with lime wedges and a cucumber, avocado and red onion salad.

Serves 6   30 minutes or less

pan-fried fish with citrus almond butter

red pepper, chicken and bean quesadillas

chicken, mushroom and asparagus stir-fry

You can substitute zucchini for the spinach if preferred.

1 tablespoon olive oil
1 lb (500g) skinless, boneless chicken breasts, thinly sliced
1 bunch green onion, sliced
4 garlic cloves, minced
1 teaspoon sambal oelek (chili paste)
3 cups sliced mushrooms (about 8 oz/250g)
1 bunch asparagus, trimmed of woody ends
  and cut into 1 inch (2.5cm) pieces
2 tablespoons sour cream
salt and freshly ground pepper
2 tablespoons lemon juice
1/3 cup finely grated, fresh parmesan cheese
1/3 cup slivered almonds, toasted (see page 22 for tips)

Heat a wok or large frying pan over medium-high heat. Add the oil and chicken and cook, stirring occasionally, for about 5 minutes or until the chicken is browned.

Add the green onion, garlic, sambal oelek and mushrooms and stir-fry, for 3 to 5 minutes or until the mushrooms are softened.

Add the asparagus and stir-fry for 2 to 3 minutes until they are bright green and crisp.

Add the remaining ingredients and stir-fry for about 1 minute or until hot. Serve immediately.

Make ahead: The stir-fry is best made just before serving.

Serving suggestion: Serve with hot pasta tossed with olive oil and lemon juice or steamed jasmine rice (see page 21 for tips).

Serves 4   30 minutes or less

chicken, mushroom and asparagus stir-fry

moroccan lamb stew with almond couscous

moroccan lamb stew
with almond couscous

Although the ingredient list may look a little lengthy, the method is simple and takes little time to prepare. Once the stew is in the oven you don't have to worry about it for a couple of hours. Lamb shoulder works best in this recipe, but if you can't find it, then use leg of lamb instead. The almond couscous side dish takes 5 minutes to prepare.

1 tablespoon olive oil, plus 1 tablespoon extra
2 1/2 lbs (1.25kg) lamb shoulder or leg,
   cut into 3/4 inch (2cm) cubes
2 cups thinly sliced onion (about 2 medium onions)
4 garlic cloves, minced
2 teaspoons ground cumin
2 teaspoons ground coriander
1 teaspoon ground ginger
1/2 teaspoon ground cinnamon
1 teaspoon sambal oelek (chili paste)
2 cups chicken broth
   (your own, see page 15, or store bought)
1/2 cup dry white wine
2/3 cup pitted prunes, halved
1/2 cup dried apricots, halved
2 tablespoons honey
salt and freshly ground pepper
1/3 cup large pitted green olives, halved, optional

almond couscous
2 cups chicken broth
   (your own, see page 15, or store bought)
2 teaspoons olive oil
2 cups couscous
salt and freshly ground pepper
1/2 cup slivered almonds, toasted (see page 22 for tips)

Grease a large, deep casserole dish. Preheat the oven to 325°F (160°C).

Heat 1 tablespoon of the oil in a large frying pan over medium-high heat. Add the lamb in 2 to 3 batches and sear for about 5 minutes or until browned; remove from the pan.

Heat the extra oil in the same frying pan over medium heat. Add the onion and cook, stirring occasionally, for about 5 minutes or until softened.

Add the garlic, spices and sambal oelek and stir for about 1 minute or until fragrant.

Put the lamb, onion mixture, broth, wine, prunes, apricots, honey and a pinch of salt and pepper into the prepared dish and stir until combined. Cook, covered, in the preheated oven for 1 hour. Remove the cover and stir. Cook, uncovered, stirring occasionally, a further 1 hour or until the lamb is tender.

Stir in the olives, cover and let stand for 10 minutes or until hot.

To make the almond couscous, heat the broth and oil in a medium frying pan over high heat until boiling. Remove from the heat and immediately stir in the couscous and a pinch of salt and pepper. Cover and let stand for 5 minutes before fluffing the couscous with a fork. Stir in the almonds. Serve with the stew.

Make ahead: The stew can be made 2 days ahead and stored in an airtight container in the fridge. Or freeze for up to 6 months. A stew made with spices always tastes better a day or two after making it, so this stew is a perfect make-ahead recipe. The couscous is best made just before serving.

Serving suggestion: Toss broccoli florets in olive oil, salt and pepper on a baking sheet and roast for about 15 minutes or until bright green and crisp.

Serves 6   ❁ make ahead

quick beef and spinach curry

quick beef and spinach curry

Curry paste can be found in Asian markets and in the Asian section of grocery stores. Naan bread can also be found in grocery stores.

1 tablespoon vegetable oil
1 lb (500g) beef rib eye steak, thinly sliced
1 1/2 tablespoons mild curry paste
14 oz (398ml) can diced tomatoes, undrained
2 cups packed baby spinach leaves
2 cups cooked chick peas (your own, see page 16,
   or 19 oz/540ml can, rinsed and drained)
1/4 cup chopped fresh mint
4 naan bread, warmed*
1/4 cup mango chutney
1/3 cup plain yogurt

Heat the oil in a large frying pan over medium-high heat. Add the beef and cook, stirring occasionally, for about 5 minutes or until browned. Remove from the pan.

Add the curry paste and cook, stirring, for about 1 minute or until fragrant.

Stir in the tomatoes and their juice and simmer, stirring occasionally, for about 10 minutes or until thickened.

Add the spinach, chick peas, mint and beef and cook for about 2 minutes until the spinach is wilted and the chick peas are hot.

Spread one side of each piece of bread with the chutney. Top with the beef mixture and yogurt.

Make ahead: This curry is best made just before serving.

* To warm the bread, wrap it in foil and place in a warm oven for about 10 minutes. Or, place on a heated grill pan or barbecue for about 2 minutes on each side until grill marks appear.

Serves 4   30 minutes or less

spicy beef and red wine stew

spicy beef and red wine stew

Chorizo sausages can be purchased from the deli section of most grocery stores and specialty food stores. The sausage is made from pork and flavoured with garlic and spices. This recipe uses the cooked, Spanish-style chorizo. The casings can be removed before cooking if preferred.

2 chorizo sausages, thinly sliced
1 tablespoon olive oil, plus 1 tablespoon extra
2 lbs (1kg) beef chuck steak, cut into 3/4 inch (2cm) cubes
2 cups thinly sliced onion (about 2 medium onions)
4 garlic cloves, minced
2 teaspoons sambal oelek (chili paste)
28 oz (796ml) can diced tomatoes, undrained
    (or 3 cups of your own stewed tomatoes, see page 13)
1 cup red wine
4 cups chopped carrot (about 5 large carrots)
salt and freshly ground pepper
2 cups cooked chick peas (your own, see page 16,
    or 19 oz/540ml can, rinsed and drained)
1/3 cup finely chopped fresh parsley
1 1/2 tablespoons finely grated lemon zest

Cook the chorizo in a large pot or Dutch oven over medium-high heat, stirring occasionally, for about 5 minutes or until lightly browned. Put the chorizo on a plate lined with paper towel. Drain any fat from the pot.

Heat 1 tablespoon of the oil in the same pot over medium-high heat. Add the beef in 2 or 3 batches and sear for about 5 minutes or until browned; remove from the pot.

Heat the extra oil in the same pot over medium-high heat. Add the onion, garlic and sambal oelek and cook, stirring occasionally, for about 5 minutes or until the onion is softened.

Add the chorizo, beef, tomatoes and their juice, wine, carrot and a pinch of salt and pepper and stir. Cover and bring to a boil. Reduce the heat to low and simmer, stirring occasionally, for about 1 3/4 hours or until the beef is tender.

Stir in the chick peas and simmer, uncovered, for 15 to 30 minutes or until the sauce is thickened.

Add the parsley and zest and stir until combined.

Make ahead: The stew can be made 3 days ahead and stored in an airtight container in the fridge. Or freeze for up to 6 months. Reheat slowly over low heat or microwave until hot.

Serving suggestion: Serve with a crusty baguette and **garden salad with blue cheese and maple dressing** (page 63) or steamed broccoli.

Serves 8   make ahead

chicken, lemon and rosemary stew

chicken, lemon and rosemary stew

For the best flavour, use juicy, sweeter lemons in this recipe.
Have lots of warm crusty bread on hand to soak up all the
wonderful sap-like sauce from the stew.

1 tablespoon olive oil
8 bone-in chicken thighs, skin removed*
6 large shallots (eshallots) thinly sliced
4 garlic cloves, minced
1 cup chicken broth (your own, see page 15, or store bought)
1/2 cup dry white wine
2 rosemary sprigs
1 lemon, quartered
1 bay leaf
salt and freshly ground pepper
2 tablespoons lemon juice
2 cups cooked white beans (your own, see page 16,
    or 19 oz/540ml can, rinsed and drained)

Preheat the oven to 350°F (180°C).

Heat the oil in a medium, deep, flame-proof casserole dish**
over medium-high heat. Add the chicken in 2 batches and sear
for 3 to 5 minutes on each side or until browned.

Return all the chicken to the same dish along with the shallots,
garlic, broth, wine, rosemary, lemon, bay leaf and a pinch of
salt and pepper. Cover and cook in the preheated oven for
45 minutes.

Stir in the juice and beans and cook, uncovered, for about 15
minutes or until the chicken is tender and cooked through.

Remove the rosemary stems, lemon and bay leaf before
serving if preferred or leave them in for a more rustic look.
Serve hot.

Make ahead: The stew can be made 3 days ahead and stored
in an airtight container in the fridge. Or freeze for up to 6
months. Reheat slowly over low heat or microwave until hot.

Serving suggestion: Toss broccoli florets, sliced carrots, olive
oil, honey and salt and pepper together in a large frying pan
or wok. Stir-fry for about 5 minutes or until the vegetables are
bright and crisp.

* To remove the skin from the chicken, moisten your fingers
and coat them liberally in salt. Pull the skin back towards the
knuckle-end, using more salt if needed to help you grip
the skin.

** If you don't have a deep, flame-proof casserole dish then
brown the chicken in a frying pan and add it to a deep
ovenproof casserole dish instead.

Serves 4   make ahead

john's sweet curried sausages

This recipe invokes a warm comforting feeling within me. My father has cooked it for me since I was a child, and today, I still love it. Make sure the curry powder you use is fresh. Also, use the best beef sausages you can or ask a butcher to make you some using nothing but pure beef. It's worth the flavour.

2 teaspoons vegetable oil, plus 2 teaspoons extra
12 good-quality thick beef sausages,
    cut into 1 inch (2.5cm) lengths
1 1/2 cups thinly sliced onion (about 1 large onion)
4 garlic cloves, minced
2 teaspoons finely grated ginger
2 tablespoons curry powder
2 cups beef broth
1 cup dark raisins
2 large apples, peeled, cored and thinly sliced
salt and freshly ground pepper
2 medium ripe bananas, sliced

Heat 2 teaspoons of the oil in a large frying pan over medium-high heat. Add the sausages and cook, stirring occasionally, for 5 to 10 minutes or until browned; remove from the pan. Drain any excess fat from the pan (if using good-quality sausages, the fat should be minimal, if any).

Heat the extra oil in the same pan over medium-high. Add the onion and cook, stirring occasionally, for about 10 minutes or until softened and lightly browned.

Add the garlic, ginger and curry powder and cook, stirring, for about 1 minute or until fragrant.

Stir in the broth and bring to a boil. Reduce the heat to medium. Add the raisins, apples, sausages and a pinch of salt and pepper. Cook, uncovered, stirring occasionally, for about 10 minutes or until the sauce is thickened and the apples are tender.

Gently stir in the bananas and cook for about 2 minutes or until hot. Serve hot.

Make ahead: The curry can be made a day ahead. As with most curries, the flavour is even better the next day. Reheat slowly over low heat or in the microwave.

Serving suggestion: Serve with steamed jasmine rice (see page 21 for tips) and a tomato and cucumber salad.

Serves 6   30 minutes or less   make ahead

john's sweet curried sausages

salmon and sweet potato patties with horseradish mayonnaise

salmon and sweet potato patties with horseradish mayonnaise

The patties can be shaped a day ahead of serving, so when you get home from work all you have to do is cook them and make a salad. Remove and discard the skin from the salmon or ask your fishmonger to do it for you.

horseradish mayonnaise
1/2 cup mayonnaise (your own, see page 21,
 or store bought)
2 tablespoons chopped fresh dill
2 tablespoons creamed horseradish

salmon and sweet potato patties
3/4 lb (375g) sweet potato (yam), peeled and chopped
1 lb (500g) salmon, diced
2 eggs
1/2 cup chopped red onion
2 garlic cloves, minced
1 cup cooked lentils (your own, see page 16,
 or 1 cup canned, rinsed and drained)
1 cup fresh breadcrumbs (see page 21 for tips)
1 tablespoon chopped fresh dill
salt and freshly ground pepper
olive oil

To make the horseradish mayonnaise, combine all the ingredients in a small bowl and set aside in the fridge until ready to use.

To make the salmon and sweet potato patties, cook the sweet potato in salted water in a medium saucepan over medium-high heat for about 10 minutes or until tender; drain well.

Put the salmon, sweet potato, eggs, onion, garlic, lentils, breadcrumbs, dill and a pinch of salt and pepper into a food processor and process until combined. Shape the mixture into 12 patties.

Heat a little oil in a large frying pan, preferably non-stick, over medium heat. Add the patties and cook for 3 to 4 minutes on each side or until golden brown and the salmon is cooked. (The patties are soft, so take care when turning them over.) Serve hot with the mayonnaise.

Make ahead: The mayonnaise and patties can be prepared a day ahead and stored in separate airtight containers in the fridge. Cook the patties just before serving.

Serving suggestion: Serve with the **garden salad** (page 63), but omit the **blue cheese and maple dressing** and drizzle with lemon vinaigrette instead.

Serves 4 to 6 ✳ make ahead

orange spiced roast chicken

Spreading spices under the skin of the chicken allows the flavour to permeate the chicken. The skin serves to keep the chicken moist and can then be discarded once the chicken is cooked. The method might sound a little complicated, but it is really very quick and easy. This method is known as "butterflying," and it helps the chicken roast evenly.

3 lbs (1.5kg) whole chicken
1/4 cup chopped fresh parsley
1 tablespoon olive oil
1 tablespoon finely grated orange zest
2 teaspoons softened butter
1/2 teaspoon ground cumin
1/2 teaspoon ground coriander
1/4 teaspoon ground cinnamon
1/2 teaspoon sambal oelek (chili paste)
salt and freshly ground pepper
2 tablespoons honey

Grease a wire rack and place it on a large baking dish lined with parchment paper. Preheat the oven to 375°F (190°C).

Rinse the chicken inside and out with cold water and pat dry with paper towel. Lay the chicken, breast side down, on a cutting board. Using sharp poultry or kitchen scissors, cut down either side of the backbone to remove it (discard the backbone or save it to add to a homemade broth). Turn the chicken over and press down lightly to flatten it. Carefully run your fingers underneath the skin of the chicken loosening it from the flesh.

Combine the parsley, oil, zest, butter, spices, sambal oelek and a pinch of salt and pepper in a small bowl.

Spread the parsley mixture evenly between the skin and the flesh of the chicken across the breast and legs (because of the chili, it is best to wear a glove for this step).

Place the chicken, breast side up, on the prepared wire rack.* Roast, uncovered, in the preheated oven for 1 1/4 hours. Cover the chicken loosely with foil if it's browning too quickly.

Brush the chicken with the honey. Cook for a further 10 minutes or until cooked and the juices run clear when the chicken is pierced around the thigh bone (or when a meat thermometer reads 180°F/82°C, when inserted into the thickest part of the thigh). Cover the chicken with foil to keep warm and let stand for 10 minutes before carving.

Barbecue Method: This chicken dish is delicious cooked on the barbecue to impart a wonderful smoky flavour. Preheat the barbecue to high, turn off one of the burners and grease the grill on the unlit side. Cook the chicken, breast side up, on the greased grill using indirect heat. Close the lid and cook for 1 to 1 1/4 hours. Cover the chicken loosely with foil if it's browning too fast. Brush with the honey and cook for about 10 minutes or until cooked through as per oven method.

Make ahead: The chicken can be prepared with the parsley mixture a day ahead. Store, covered, in the fridge. Let stand at room temperature for 30 minutes before roasting.

Serving suggestion: Serve with garlic mashed potatoes and grilled zucchini.

* To prevent the skin of the chicken from shrinking back as it cooks, use some toothpicks or skewers to secure the skin before cooking, if desired

Serves 4   make ahead

orange spiced roast chicken

ginger, soy and citrus salmon

If you prefer things a little spicy, then add some chopped fresh chilies or dried chilies to the marinade.

1/4 cup salt-reduced soy sauce
1/4 cup rice vinegar
2 tablespoons finely grated lime zest
1 tablespoon finely grated fresh ginger
1 tablespoon olive oil
1 tablespoon packed brown sugar
1 1/2 lbs (750g) salmon side, cut into 6 pieces
3 limes, halved crossways

Combine soy sauce, vinegar, zest, ginger, oil and sugar in a resealable plastic bag or a large, shallow dish and mix to combine. Add the salmon and mix to combine. Marinate in the fridge for 1 to 3 hours.

Preheat a barbecue or grill pan to medium-high and then grease.

Drain the salmon from the marinade and discard the marinade. Cook the salmon on the preheated barbecue for about 3 minutes on each side, depending on the thickness of the salmon, until just cooked; do not overcook.

Cook the limes with the salmon, cut side down, on the same grill for about 5 minutes or until grill marks appear. Serve with the salmon for drizzling.

Make ahead: The salmon can be marinated 1 to 3 hours ahead and stored, covered, in the fridge.

Serving suggestion: Serve with fresh egg noodles and stir-fried Shanghai bok choy.

Serves 6   make ahead

red pork curry

Coconut milk and Thai red curry paste are available in the Asian section of most grocery stores or in Asian markets. The red curry paste, although it may look fiery, isn't as hot as the green curry paste that is so popular in Thai curries.

1 tablespoon peanut oil
1 lb (500g) pork tenderloin, thinly sliced
4 garlic cloves, minced
2 teaspoons finely chopped fresh ginger
1 1/2 tablespoons Thai red curry paste
14 oz (398ml) can light coconut milk
2 tablespoons peanut butter
2 tablespoons Thai sweet chili sauce
2 teaspoons fish sauce
2 teaspoons packed brown sugar
3 cups chopped butternut squash (about 1 lb/500g)
1 cup (4 oz/125g) sugar snap peas, trimmed
1/4 cup cilantro (coriander) leaves
2 tablespoons coarsely chopped fresh basil
2 tablespoons lime juice
3 tablespoons peanuts, toasted and coarsely chopped
    (see page 22 for tips), optional

Heat a wok or a large frying pan over medium-high heat. Add the oil and pork and stir-fry for about 5 minutes or until the pork is browned. Remove the pork from the wok and set aside.

Add the garlic, ginger and curry paste and stir-fry for about 1 minute or until fragrant. Reduce the heat to medium.

Stir in the coconut milk, peanut butter, sauces and sugar. Add the squash and simmer, covered, stirring occasionally, for about 10 minutes or until the squash is tender but not mushy.

Add the pork, peas, cilantro, basil and juice and cook, uncovered, stirring occasionally, for about 3 minutes or until the peas are bright green and crisp.

Sprinkle with the peanuts just before serving.

Make ahead: The curry is best made just before serving.

Serving suggestion: Serve the curry with jasmine rice (see page 21 for tips).

Serves 4   30 minutes or less

ginger, soy and citrus salmon

red pork curry

seafood sun-dried tomato pasta

seafood sun-dried tomato pasta

Sun-dried tomato pesto is available in jars in grocery and specialty food stores.

4 cups bow tie pasta
3/4 lb (375g) large scallops
1 lb (500g) large raw shrimp, peeled and deveined
    (3/4 lb/375g peeled weight)
2 teaspoons olive oil
2 teaspoons butter
1 cup finely chopped onion (about 1 medium onion)
4 garlic cloves, minced
1 1/2 teaspoons sambal oelek (chili paste)
1/2 cup dry white wine
1/3 cup sun-dried tomato pesto
1 cup frozen peas
1/4 cup shredded fresh basil
2 tablespoons lemon juice
salt and freshly ground pepper

Cook the pasta in boiling salted water in a large pot or Dutch oven, stirring occasionally, for about 12 minutes or until al dente. Drain well, reserving 1/4 cup of the pasta water.

While the pasta is cooking, place the scallops and shrimp on a baking sheet lined with paper towel. Place more paper towel on top and press down lightly to absorb any excess moisture.

Heat the oil in a large frying pan over high heat. Add the scallops and cook, for about 2 minutes on each side or until almost cooked; do not overcook. Remove from the pan and set aside.

Add the shrimp to the same pan and cook, stirring occasionally, for about 3 minutes or until just cooked; do not overcook. Remove from the pan and set aside with the scallops.

Heat the butter in the same pan over medium heat. Add the onion, garlic and sambal oelek and cook, stirring occasionally, for about 5 minutes or until the onion is softened.

Add the wine and cook, for about 3 minutes or until reduced by about half.

Add the pesto and peas and stir for about 3 minutes or until the peas are hot.

Return the scallops and shrimp to the pan. Add the basil, juice, reserved pasta water, pasta and salt and pepper and stir until hot and well combined. Serve hot.

Make ahead: This dish is best made just before serving.

Serving suggestion: Serve with garlic bread and a glass of crisp white wine.

Serves 4   30 minutes or less

spaghetti with tomatoes and pine nuts

spaghetti with tomatoes and pine nuts

As with most of the recipes I have used chili in, adjust the chili to suit your taste and if you like things spicy, go ahead and add more; I always like to.

garlic crumbs
1 tablespoon olive oil
2 garlic cloves, minced
1 cup fresh breadcrumbs (see page 21 for tips)

spaghetti with tomatoes and pine nuts
1 tablespoon olive oil
4 garlic cloves, minced
1 teaspoon sambal oelek (chili paste)
1/2 cup red wine
3 cups stewed tomatoes (your own, see page 13, or 28 oz/796ml can, undrained)
2/3 cup pine nuts, toasted (see page 22 for tips)
2/3 cup finely grated, fresh parmesan cheese
1/2 cup chopped fresh parsley
salt and freshly ground pepper
3/4 lb (375g) spaghetti

To make the garlic crumbs, heat the oil and garlic in a medium frying pan over medium-low heat and cook, stirring occasionally, for 1 to 3 minutes or until the garlic is softened and fragrant. Stir in the breadcrumbs and cook, stirring constantly, for about 5 minutes or until crisp and golden. Spoon the breadcrumb mixture into a dish and set aside.

To make the spaghetti with tomatoes and pine nuts, heat the oil and garlic in the same pan over medium-low heat and cook, stirring occasionally, for 1 to 3 minutes or until the garlic is softened and fragrant. Stir in the sambal oelek.

Increase the heat to medium-high and add the wine and tomatoes. Cook, stirring occasionally, for 5 to 10 minutes or until thickened slightly.

Stir in the pine nuts, parmesan cheese, parsley and a pinch of salt and pepper.

While the sauce is simmering, cook the spaghetti in boiling salted water in a large pot or Dutch oven, stirring occasionally, for 12 to 15 minutes or until al dente. Drain well and return to the same pot.

Add the tomato mixture and toss to combine. Sprinkle individual servings with the breadcrumb mixture. Serve immediately.

Make ahead: The garlic crumbs can be made a day ahead and stored in an airtight container in a cool, dry place, but they are best made just before serving.

Serving suggestion: Serve with a salad of fresh spinach leaves tossed with cooked sliced mushrooms and sprinkle with goat cheese; drizzle with balsamic dressing.

Serves 4   30 minutes or less

desserts and
other sweet things

Sweet delights to tempt and nourish. Take some time and create a perfect ending to a sumptuous meal or put some coffee on, kick off your shoes and share some cake and cookies with a friend.

pavlovas with raspberries and lemon curd sauce

A pavlova is a crisp and slightly chewy meringue base that's traditionally topped with whipped cream and fruit. My mum has been making the best pavlovas for parties and barbecues since I can remember. To me, a pavlova layered with fresh ripe fruit says "summer".

3 egg whites
3/4 cup granulated sugar
1 1/2 cups fresh raspberries

lemon curd sauce
1/2 cup granulated sugar
1/3 cup lemon juice
3 eggs
1/4 cup butter, cut into pieces

Trace 6, 3 inch (8cm) circles, about 1 1/2 inches (3.5cm) apart, on a piece of parchment paper. Place the parchment paper, circle side down, onto a large baking sheet. Preheat the oven to 250°F (120°C).

Using an electric mixer, beat the egg whites in a medium, clean bowl until soft peaks form. Gradually add the sugar a little at a time, beating well after each addition until stiff peaks form.

Spoon the mixture into each circle on the prepared baking sheet and spread evenly inside the circles, making a hollow in the centre of each so the raspberries have somewhere to nest once the pavlovas are cooked. Bake in the preheated oven for about 1 1/4 hours or until the pavlovas are dry. Turn the oven off and let the pavlovas cool in the oven with the door slightly ajar (this ensures the pavlovas cool down slowly).

To make the lemon curd sauce, whisk the sugar, juice and eggs in a medium bowl until well combined. Place the bowl over a small saucepan of simmering water, ensuring that the bottom of the bowl does not touch the water. Stir constantly for 5 to 10 minutes or until thickened and the mixture coats the back of a spoon.

Remove from the heat and stir in the butter a little at a time until it is melted before adding more butter.

Top each pavlova with raspberries and drizzle with the warm sauce. Serve immediately.

Make ahead: The pavlovas can be made a day ahead and stored in an airtight container in a cool, dry place. Do not store them in the fridge.

Serves 6　　　　　　　　　　　　　　　　　※ make ahead

banana and macadamia cake with maple sauce

I love this cake because it is so easy to make and it's really moist, as most banana cakes are. You can use another sort of nut in place of macadamia nuts if you prefer. Walnuts or hazelnuts make a delicious substitute. This cake is best served warm with the warm sauce.

1 3/4 cup all-purpose flour
1 tablespoon baking powder
1 teaspoon baking soda
3/4 cup macadamia nuts, toasted and chopped
　　(see page 22 for tips)
1/2 cup butter
1/2 cup packed brown sugar
1 teaspoon vanilla extract
1 1/2 cups mashed over-ripe bananas
　　(about 3 large bananas)
1 egg
3 tablespoons milk

maple sauce
1/3 cup maple syrup
3 tablespoons water
3 tablespoons butter

Grease a 9 inch (23cm) deep, round cake pan (such as a spring form pan) and line the base and side with parchment paper. Preheat the oven to 350°F (180°C).

Sift the flour, baking powder and soda into a large bowl. Add the nuts and stir until well combined. Make a well in the centre of the flour mixture.

Stir the butter and sugar in a small saucepan over medium heat until the butter is melted and the sugar is dissolved. Add the butter mixture and the remaining ingredients to the flour mixture and stir until combined.

Pour the mixture into the prepared pan. Bake on the centre rack in the preheated oven for about 40 minutes or until a skewer inserted into the centre of the cake comes out clean. Let stand in the pan for 10 minutes before turning out onto a wire rack. Cover the cake to keep it warm.

To make the maple sauce, combine the maple syrup and water in a small saucepan over medium heat. Boil gently for 3 to 5 minutes or until thickened slightly. Remove from the heat and whisk in the butter a little at a time until it is melted.

Immediately drizzle the warm sauce over the warm cake. Cut the cake into 8 to 10 pieces. Serve warm.

Make ahead: The cake and sauce are best made just before serving. However, you can make the cake a day ahead and store, covered with plastic wrap, in a cool, dry place. Make the sauce a day ahead and store in an airtight container in the fridge. Just before serving, heat the cake in the microwave until warm. Heat the sauce in a microwave-safe dish until warm; drizzle over the cake.

Serves 8 to 10　　　　　　　　　　　　　　※ make ahead

pavlovas with raspberries and lemon curd sauce

banana and macadamia cake with maple sauce

apple and ginger crostata

A crostata, or galette, its French name, is a free-formed, rustic-looking pie. Granny Smith apples are best for this recipe.

1 1/2 cups all-purpose flour
1 teaspoon ground cinnamon
salt
3/4 cup cold butter, cut into cubes
2 egg yolks
3 tablespoons iced water, approximately

1/2 cup pecans, toasted (see page 22 for tips)
2 tablespoons granulated sugar
1 tablespoon all-purpose flour
3 tablespoons thinly sliced crystallized ginger
5 medium green apples, peeled,
   cored and thinly sliced (about 5 cups)
2 tablespoons packed brown sugar
1 egg yolk, lightly beaten

To make the pastry, put the flour, cinnamon and a small pinch of salt in a food processor and process until well combined. Add the butter and process until the mixture resembles course crumbs. Add the yolks and enough water to make the ingredients just come together (do not over process or you will toughen the pastry).

Turn the dough out onto a lightly floured surface and press to form a disk-shape. Cover with plastic wrap and place in the fridge for 30 minutes.

Lightly grease a large baking sheet. Preheat the oven to 375°F (190°C).

Roll the pastry out on a lightly floured surface until 14 inches (36cm) in diameter (the pastry doesn't have to be in a perfect circle; this is a rustic-looking dish, remember). Carefully lift the pastry onto the prepared baking sheet (you will have pastry hanging over the sides).

To make the apple filling, put the pecans, granulated sugar and flour in a food processor and process until finely chopped. Sprinkle the mixture over the pastry, leaving a 2 1/2 inch (6cm) border around the edge.

Scatter the ginger over the pecan mixture. Arrange the apple slices over the ginger and sprinkle with the brown sugar. Fold the excess pastry edge over the filling and brush the pastry with the yolk.

Bake, uncovered, on the bottom rack in the preheated oven for 45 to 50 minutes or until golden brown. Cut into 8 wedges and serve warm.

Make ahead: The pastry can be prepared a day ahead, wrapped in plastic wrap and stored in the fridge. The crostata is best made just before serving.

Serving suggestion: Serve with your favourite ice cream.

Serves 8

apple and ginger crostata

pistachio citrus biscotti

Substitute other nuts such as almonds or macadamia nuts for the pistachios if preferred.

1 3/4 cups all-purpose flour
2/3 cup granulated sugar
1/2 teaspoon baking powder
1 tablespoon finely grated orange zest
1 tablespoon finely grated lemon zest
1/4 cup softened butter
2 eggs
1 1/2 teaspoons vanilla extract
3/4 cup shelled pistachio nuts, coarsely chopped

Line a baking sheet with parchment paper. Preheat the oven to 350°F (180°C).

Put the flour, sugar, baking powder and both zests into a food processor and process until well combined.

Add the butter and process until the mixture resembles fine crumbs.

Add the eggs, vanilla and nuts and process until the mixture is starting to come together.

Turn the mixture out onto a lightly floured surface, knead and press into a dough. Divide the dough into 2 equal portions and shape each portion into 8 inch (20cm) logs. Place on the prepared baking sheet, about 3 inches apart.

Bake on the centre rack in the preheated oven for about 35 minutes or until golden. Let stand for about 30 minutes or until cool.

Preheat the oven to 325°F (160°C). Cut each log into 1/2 inch (1cm) slices. Place the slices, cut side down, in a single layer on the same baking sheet. Bake, on the centre rack, in the preheated oven, turning once during cooking, for about 25 minutes or until they are dry and golden. Transfer to a wire rack to cool completely before storing.

Make ahead: The biscotti can be made 4 days ahead and stored in an airtight container in a cool, dry place.

Serving suggestion: Serve with coffee or dessert wine.

Makes about 32 pieces   make ahead

pistachio citrus biscotti

baked lemon lime puddings

baked lemon lime puddings

This simple, old-fashioned dessert has a light sponge top with a smooth, tart lemon curd on the bottom.

3 egg yolks
1/2 cup granulated sugar, plus 1/2 cup extra
1 cup milk
2 tablespoons melted butter
1 tablespoon finely grated lemon zest
1 tablespoon finely grated lime zest
3 tablespoons lemon juice
2 tablespoons lime juice
1/2 cup all-purpose flour
1 teaspoon baking powder
3 egg whites

Grease 6, 1 cup (8 oz/250ml) capacity ramekins and place them in a shallow, large baking dish or roasting pan. Preheat the oven to 350°F (180°C).

Using an electric mixer, beat the egg yolks and 1/2 cup of the sugar in a small bowl until thick and creamy. Scrape into a large bowl.

Add the milk, butter, both zests, both juices, flour and baking powder and stir gently until combined.

Using an electric mixer, with clean beaters, beat the egg whites in a small, clean bowl until soft peaks form. Gradually add the extra sugar a little at a time, beating well after each addition until stiff peaks form.

Fold the egg white mixture into the egg yolk mixture in 2 batches. Pour into the prepared ramekins. Add enough hot water into the baking dish to come halfway up the side of the ramekins. Bake in the preheated oven for about 30 minutes or until the puddings are just set.

Make ahead: The puddings are best made just before serving.

Serves 6

date, apple and walnut strudel

date, apple and walnut strudel

The crisp tartness of Granny Smith apples are perfect for a strudel.

3 medium green apples, peeled
    and thinly sliced (about 3 cups)
1/2 cup chopped dates
1/2 cup walnuts, toasted and finely chopped
    (see page 22 for tips)
1/2 cup fine dry breadcrumbs
1/4 cup granulated sugar, plus 1 teaspoon extra
2 tablespoons honey
1 teaspoon ground ginger
1/4 teaspoon ground cinnamon
8 sheets phyllo pastry, thawed
2 tablespoons melted butter, plus 1 teaspoon extra
1 tablespoon milk

Grease a large baking sheet. Preheat the oven to 350°F (180°C).

Combine the apples, dates, walnuts, breadcrumbs, 1/4 cup of sugar, honey and spices in a large bowl.

Place a sheet of phyllo pastry on a smooth surface, with one short end closest to you. (Cover the remaining pastry with a damp tea towel to prevent it from drying out.) Brush the pastry with a little melted butter. Layer it with another sheet of pastry and brush with a little milk. Repeat with the remaining pastry, alternating between brushing with butter and milk.

Arrange the apple mixture across the short end of the pastry closest to you. Leaving the ends open, roll up firmly to enclose the filling. (Just poke back in any filling that comes out the ends.) Place on the prepared baking sheet, seam side down. Brush with the extra butter and sprinkle with the extra sugar.

Bake on the centre rack in the preheated oven for about 45 minutes or until golden and crisp. Cut into 8 slices to serve. Serve warm.

Make ahead: The strudel is best made just before serving. The filling can be prepared 1 hour before baking and stored, covered, at room temperature.

Serving suggestion: Serve with a low-fat ice cream or plain yogurt flavoured with a little honey.

Serves 8

pineapple passionfruit sorbet

cornflake cranberry cookies

pear and blue cheese on toast

blueberries and oranges with zabaglione

pineapple passionfruit sorbet

Passionfruit is a tropical fruit with a sweet, tart flavour and a fresh, almost perfume-like aroma when cut. Passionfruit can be found in many grocery stores. Choose heavy passionfruit with a deep purple colour. You will need about 6 for this recipe.

1/2 cup granulated sugar
1 cup water
2 1/2 cups pineapple juice
1/2 cup passionfruit pulp*
3 egg whites
coconut for decoration (optional)

Stir the sugar and water in a medium saucepan over medium heat until the sugar is dissolved. Boil gently, uncovered, for about 10 minutes or until the mixture is thickened slightly; remove from the heat.

Add the juice and passionfruit and stir until well combined. Pour the mixture into a medium, shallow baking dish. Cover and freeze for about 3 to 5 hours or until just set.

Scrape the mixture into a food processor and working quickly to prevent it from melting, add the egg whites and process until smooth. Pour the mixture into a 9 x 5 x 3 inch (23 x 13 x 8cm) loaf pan. Cover and freeze for 8 hours or overnight until set.

To serve, scoop the sorbet into individual serving dishes or glasses. Serve immediately.

Make ahead: The sorbet is best made a day ahead to allow it to freeze. It can be made a week ahead, covered, and stored in the freezer.

* To remove the pulp from the passionfruit, cut them in half crossways and scoop out the juice and seeds into a small bowl.

Serves 6 to 8   make ahead

pear and blue cheese on toast

It's nice to serve something a little different for after dinner instead of the usual sweet dessert. This recipe is perfect for serving at the end of the meal with port or dessert wine. Freezing the cheese makes it easier to grate.

8 oz (250g) blue cheese
   (use a creamy cheese such as cambozola)
1 muesli or fruit and nut loaf, cut into 1/4 inch
   (6mm) thick slices (you will need about 24 slices)
3 medium ripe pears, peeled and thinly sliced

Divide the cheese in half and wrap half in plastic wrap. Freeze for about 1 hour or until firm. Leave the remaining cheese to soften at room temperature.

Lightly grease a baking sheet. Preheat the broiler. Arrange the bread in a single layer on the prepared baking sheet. Toast under the preheated broiler for about 2 minutes on each side or until golden.

Spread one side of each slice of toast with the softened blue cheese. Arrange pear slices over the cheese. Grate the frozen cheese over the pear, place under the preheated broiler for about 2 minutes or until the cheese is melted. Serve warm.

Make ahead: The toasts are best made just before serving.

Serving suggestion: This recipe is perfect served with a glass of port, Muscat or dessert wine. It also makes a nice lunch; serve with a fresh leafy green salad.

Serves 8   30 minutes or less

cornflake cranberry cookies

These cookies are a favourite of my niece, Emily. They were a favourite of mine growing up too, and today they still are. My mum always uses sultanas when she makes them, but I use dried cranberries because I like their chewy texture.

1/2 cup softened butter
1/2 cup granulated sugar
1 egg
1 teaspoon vanilla extract
1 cup all-purpose flour
2 teaspoons baking powder
2/3 cup dried cranberries (or craisins)
2 1/2 cups cornflakes

Line 2 baking sheets with parchment paper. Preheat the oven to 350°F (180°C). Using an electric mixer, beat the butter and sugar in a small, deep bowl until light and fluffy. Add the egg and vanilla and beat until well combined.

Add the flour, baking powder and cranberries and stir until combined.

Place the cornflakes in a medium, shallow dish. Drop tablespoons of the mixture into the cornflakes. Roll the mixture in the cornflakes until well coated. Place on the prepared baking sheets about 2 inches (5cm) apart. Bake on the centre and top racks in the preheated oven for about 15 minutes or until the bottom of the cookies are golden (swap baking sheets around halfway through cooking). Repeat with the remaining mixture and cornflakes. Transfer the cookies to a wire rack to cool. Cool completely before storing.

Make ahead: The cookies can be made 3 days ahead and stored in an airtight container in a cool, dry place.

Makes about 28   make ahead

blueberries and oranges with zabaglione

Traditionally, zabaglione, a light egg custard, is made with Marsala. Here I have used an orange liqueur.

3 cups blueberries (fresh or frozen, thawed)
4 oranges, segmented (see page 10 for tips)
2 tablespoons orange liqueur (such as Cointreau)
1 tablespoon granulated sugar

zabaglione
4 egg yolks
1/3 cup granulated sugar
3 tablespoons orange liqueur (such as Cointreau)

Gently stir the blueberries, oranges, liqueur and sugar in a medium bowl. Cover with plastic wrap and store in the fridge for 1 to 3 hours, stirring occasionally, to allow the flavours to develop.

To make the zabaglione, combine the yolks and sugar in a medium, heatproof bowl. Using an electric hand mixer, beat until the mixture is thick and pale. Place the bowl over a small saucepan of simmering water, ensuring that the bottom of the bowl is not sitting in the water. Continue beating the mixture, adding 2 teaspoons of the liqueur at a time until all the liqueur is added and the mixture is thickened.

To serve, spoon some of the blueberry mixture into individual serving glasses or dishes and drizzle with the zabaglione. Serve immediately.

Make ahead: The blueberries and oranges can be made a day ahead and stored in an airtight container in the fridge; stir before serving. The zabaglione is best made just before serving.

Serves 4 to 6

tea poached peaches with panna cotta

tea poached peaches
with panna cotta

Choose ripe fresh peaches without any blemishes. Panna cotta is a smooth, lightly set custard dessert. Traditionally, this Italian dessert is made with whole cream. In this recipe I have reduced the fat a little by using light cream. Whole star anise can be found in the spice section of most grocery stores or in Asian markets.

panna cotta
2 1/2 cups light cream (10% MF)
2 1/4 teaspoons gelatin (or one envelope)
1/4 cup honey
1 teaspoon vanilla extract

tea poached peaches
2 cups prepared green tea
1/4 cup packed brown sugar
1 star anise
4 medium ripe peaches

To make the panna cotta, grease 4, 1/2 cup (4 oz/125ml) capacity moulds and place them on a baking sheet.

Place 1/4 cup of the cream in a small saucepan. Sprinkle with the gelatin and let stand for 5 minutes. Stir over medium-low heat for about 5 minutes or until the gelatin is completely dissolved. Remove from the heat.

Add the remaining cream, honey and vanilla and stir until well combined. Pour into the prepared moulds, cover and place in the fridge for 8 hours or overnight until set.

To make the tea poached peaches, combine the tea, sugar and star anise in a medium saucepan and stir over medium heat until the sugar is dissolved.

Add the peaches and cook, gently turning them occasionally, for 10 to 15 minutes or until the peaches are tender. (Cooking times may vary according to the ripeness of the peaches; test if the peaches are cooked by inserting a small sharp knife into one.) Pour the peaches, with the tea mixture, into a large bowl and let cool; discard the star anise. Peel away and discard the skin from the peaches. Return them to the tea mixture. Cover and place in the fridge for 8 hours or overnight, gently stirring occasionally.

To serve, turn the panna cotta out of the moulds onto 4 individual serving plates. Add a peach and spoonfuls of the tea mixture. Serve cold.

Make ahead: Both the panna cotta and the peaches are best made a day ahead and stored, covered, in the fridge.

Serves 4   make ahead

liqueur popsicles

liqueur popsicles

If you prefer to make a non-alcoholic variation of these, simply leave out the alcohol; they are still delicious and perfect for a warm summer's day or evening. To produce the best result, it is important to use a blender and not a food processor.

mango pineapple with orange liqueur

2 fresh mangoes, peeled and chopped
   (or 14 oz/398ml can, drained)
1/2 ripe pineapple, peeled and chopped
1 cup pineapple juice
1/4 cup orange liqueur (such as Cointreau)
12 x 1/3 cup (2 1/2 oz/75ml) capacity moulds
   (such as paper Dixie cups)
12 popsicle sticks

Put the mangoes, pineapple, juice and liqueur into a blender and blend until smooth.

Place the moulds on a baking sheet. Divide the pineapple mixture into each mould. Freeze for 1 hour.

Place a popsicle stick in the centre of each mould. Freeze for 8 hours or overnight until set.

To serve, peel away the paper moulds. If you are using plastic moulds, set them in warm water for 30 to 60 seconds to make them easy to remove. Serve immediately.

berry lime

1/2 cup lime juice
1/2 cup water
1/2 cup granulated sugar
1 1/4 lbs (600g) frozen mixed berries
1/4 cup tequila
12 x 1/3 cup (2 1/2 oz/75ml) capacity moulds
   (such as paper Dixie cups)
12 popsicle sticks

Stir juice, water and sugar in a large saucepan over medium heat until the sugar is dissolved. Boil gently, uncovered, for 5 minutes or until thickened slightly.

Stir in the berries and cook, stirring occasionally, for 5 to 10 minutes or until thawed.

Put the berry mixture and tequila into a blender and blend until smooth.

Press the mixture through a fine metal sieve into a medium bowl; discard the seeds.

Place the moulds on a baking sheet. Divide the berry mixture into each mould. Freeze for 1 hour.

Place a popsicle stick in the centre of each mould. Freeze for 8 hours or overnight until set.

To serve, peel away the paper moulds. If you are using plastic moulds, set them in warm water for 30 to 60 seconds to make them easy to remove. Serve immediately.

Make ahead: The popsicles are best made a day ahead to give them time to freeze properly. They can be made 2 weeks ahead and stored covered in the freezer.

Serving suggestion: These are fun to serve to your guests for dessert on a hot summer's night.

Makes 12   ❄ make ahead

strawberry chocolate ice cream cones

strawberry chocolate
ice cream cones

Frozen strawberries work best in this recipe. It is important to use a blender first and then a food processor, as the recipe stipulates, to produce the best result. If you have an ice cream maker, freeze the mixture according to the manufacturer's instructions.

1 cup granulated sugar
1/4 cup water
1 1/2 lbs (750g) frozen strawberries
8 egg yolks
2 teaspoons vanilla extract
2 cups light cream (10% MF), plus 2 cups extra
3 1/2 oz (100g) good-quality dark chocolate, chopped
3 1/2 oz (100g) good-quality milk chocolate, chopped
12 ice cream cones for serving

Put the sugar and water in a large saucepan and stir over medium heat until the sugar is dissolved. Add the strawberries and bring to a boil. Boil gently, uncovered, stirring occasionally, for about 15 minutes or until the strawberries are broken down and the liquid is thickened slightly; set aside.

Whisk the egg yolks and vanilla in a medium bowl. Heat 2 cups of cream in a medium saucepan over medium-high heat until bubbles form around the side of the pan. Whisk 1/2 cup of the hot cream into the egg yolk mixture to warm them. Add that mixture back into the remaining hot cream. Stir constantly on medium-low heat for 5 to 10 minutes or until the mixture is thickened and coats the back of a spoon. Pour into a medium bowl and cover the surface of the custard mixture with plastic wrap. Place in the fridge for about 2 hours or until cooled.

Heat the extra cream in a large saucepan over medium-high heat until bubbles form around the side of the pan. Remove from the heat, add both of the chocolates and stir until melted. Stir in the strawberry mixture. Pour into a large bowl and cover with plastic wrap. Place in the fridge for about 2 hours or until cooled.

Add the custard mixture to the strawberry mixture and stir until well combined. Put the mixture into a blender in batches and blend until smooth. Pour into a large, shallow baking dish. Cover and freeze for about 3 hours or until just set. (If the mixture sets too hard at this stage, then let stand at room temperature for 15 to 30 minutes or until soft enough to easily scoop.)*

Spoon the ice cream mixture into a food processor in batches and process until very smooth. Pour into a 9 x 13 inch (23 x 32.5cm) baking dish or 2, 9 x 5 x 3 inch (23 x 13 x 8cm) loaf pans. Cover and freeze for 8 hours or overnight until frozen. (If the mixture sets too hard to scoop, let it stand at room temperature for 15 to 30 minutes or until softened slightly.)*

Make ahead: The ice cream is best made a day ahead. It can be made a month ahead and stored in an airtight container in the freezer.

* Freezing times are approximate because freezers differ in their freezing ability. This recipe was tested in 3 different freezers and each one froze the ice cream in different times.

Serves 12   make ahead

dark chocolate brownies

Granted, the word "brownie" does not equate with being particularly healthful. But did you know there are health benefits of good dark chocolate? It contains antioxidants, which is my excuse for indulging in it from time to time. This brownie recipe is quite decadent (as most brownie recipes are), so, really, you only need a small piece. I used Lindt chocolate containing 70% cocoa in this recipe.

1 cup butter, cut into pieces
10 1/2 oz (300g) good-quality dark chocolate, chopped, plus 3 1/2 oz (100g) extra, chopped
2 cups granulated sugar
5 eggs
1 cup all-purpose flour
1/2 teaspoon baking powder
1/2 cup cocoa powder
salt

Grease a 9 x 13 inch (23 x 32.5cm) baking pan and line the base and sides with parchment paper. Preheat the oven to 350°F (180°C).

Stir the butter and 10 1/2 oz (300g) of the chocolate in a large saucepan over medium heat until both are just melted. Remove from the heat.

Add the sugar and eggs and stir until well combined.

Sift the flour, baking powder, cocoa and a pinch of salt into the chocolate mixture and stir until well combined.

Stir in the extra chocolate and spread the mixture into the prepared pan.

Bake, on the centre rack, in the preheated oven for 35 to 40 minutes or until just firm. (It will set more as it cools.) Let cool in the pan. Cover and store in the fridge until ready to serve. Cut into 20 to 30 pieces.

Make ahead: The brownies can be made 5 days ahead and stored, well covered, in the fridge.

Serving suggestion: Serve with a really good cup of coffee, a nice pot of tea or a glass of ice cold milk.

Makes 20 to 30 pieces   make ahead

dark chocolate brownies